When Trauma Wounds

When Trauma Wounds

Pathways to Healing and Hope

Karen A. McClintock

WHEN TRAUMA WOUNDS
Pathways to Healing and Hope

Copyright © 2019 Fortress Press, an imprint of 1517 Media. All rights reserved. Except for brief quotations in critical articles or reviews, no part of this book may be reproduced in any manner without prior written permission from the publisher. Email copyright@1517.media or write to Permissions, Fortress Press, PO Box 1209, Minneapolis, MN 55440-1209.

All biblical references in this book come from the New Revised Standard Version.

Cover design: Rob Dewey

Print ISBN: 978-1-5064-3425-4
eBook ISBN: 978-1-5064-3426-1

The paper used in this publication meets the minimum requirements of American National Standard for Information Sciences — Permanence of Paper for Printed Library Materials, ANSI Z329.48-1984.

Manufactured in the U.S.A.

Contents

Series Preface		vii
Acknowledgments		ix
Introduction		1

Part One: Understanding Trauma

Chapter 1	What Is Trauma?	9
Chapter 2	Trauma's Aftermath	31
Chapter 3	Disrupted Moods and Behaviors	47
Chapter 4	Trauma's Damaged Relationships	61

Part Two: Types of Trauma

Chapter 5	When Trust Is Betrayed: Child Sexual Abuse Trauma	83
Chapter 6	When Uprooted: Immigration Heartbreak	103
Chapter 7	When Death Comes Suddenly: Gun Violence	115

Part Three: Pathways to Hope and Healing

Chapter 8	Becoming Spiritually Whole Again	133
Chapter 9	Next Steps in Healing	145
Chapter 10	Rediscovering Hope	157
Notes		167

Series Preface

MY MOST sincere wish is that the Living with Hope series will offer comfort, wisdom—and hope—to individuals facing life's most common and intimate challenges. Books in the series tackle complex problems such as addiction, parenting, unemployment, pregnancy loss, serious illness, trauma, and grief and encourage individuals, their families, and those who care for them. The series is bound together by a common message for those who are dealing with significant issues: you are not alone. There is hope.

This series offers first-person perspectives and insights from authors who know personally what it is like to face these struggles. As companions and guides, series contributors share personal experiences, offer valuable research from trusted experts, and suggest questions to help readers process their own responses and explore possible next steps. With empathy and honesty, these accessible volumes reassure individuals they are not alone in their pain, fear, or confusion.

The series is also a valuable resource for pastoral and spiritual care providers in faith-based settings. Parish pastors, lay ministers, chaplains, counselors, and other staff and volunteers can draw on these volumes to offer skilled and compassionate guidance to individuals in need of hope.

Each title in this series is offered with prayer for the reader's journey—one of discovery, further challenges, and transformation. You are not alone. There is hope.

Beth Ann Gaede, Series Editor

Titles in the Living with Hope Series

Nurturing Hope: Christian Pastoral Care in the Twenty-First Century (Lynne M. Baab)

Dignity and Grace: Wisdom for Caregivers and Those Living with Dementia (Janet L. Ramsey)

Jobs Lost, Faith Found: A Spiritual Resource for the Unemployed (Mary C. Lindberg)

They Don't Come with Instructions: Cries, Wisdom, and Hope for Parenting Children with Developmental Challenges (Hollie M. Holt-Woehl)

True Connection: Using the NAME IT Model to Heal Relationships (George Faller and Heather P. Wright)

Waiting for Good News: Living with Chronic and Serious Illness (Sally L. Wilke)

Carrying Them with Us: Living through Pregnancy or Infant Loss (David M. Engelstad and Catherine A. Malotky)

A Grief Received: What to Do When Loss Leaves You Empty-Handed (JL Gerhardt)

When Trauma Wounds: Pathways to Healing and Hope (Karen A. McClintock)

Addiction and Recovery: A Spiritual Pilgrimage (Martha Postlethwaite)

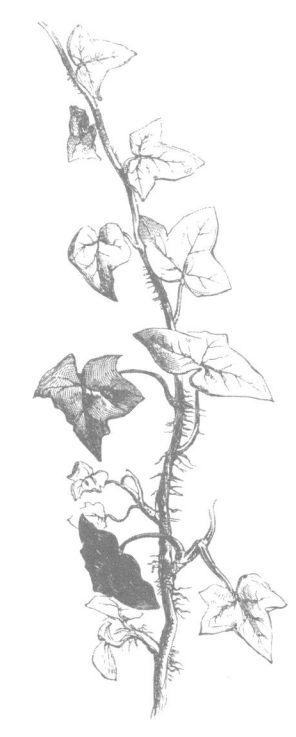

Acknowledgments

THIS BOOK is written to thank countless individuals who have trusted me to treat their traumatic wounds with tender care while offering acceptance and hope. It is written for personal friends whose lives were once so disrupted by trauma that they face daily challenges I have not had to face. It is written in the belief that life is sacred and that nothing justifies human sacrifice or suffering. As trauma victims become survivors, they show us ways to create a more just, loving, nonviolent, and resilient world. It has been a great honor to accompany them.

Introduction

On a Tuesday morning I was sitting at my office desk shuffling folders, preparing for the week ahead. My draft of the Sunday bulletin needed work, but "it'll do," I thought, and pushed it aside to watch a noisy blue jay outside my window in the courtyard. The sky was gray. In California's central valley the fog rolls in almost every fall morning. By noon, however, I could count on sunshine.

As I was turning my thoughts toward a sermon on Jesus's encounter with the leper, the phone rang. I heard a frantic voice on the other end of the line and couldn't recognize it.

"Hello, Karen," she said, as if we knew each other. "I know this is very awkward, but my name is Sarah, and I work for Child Protective Services. I have a situation I think you could best handle for us. We have an eight-year-old girl whose father is in prison and whose mother drove her car off the side of a winding mountain road and died this morning. I'm on my way to the school to pick her up. I don't feel comfortable telling her this news, and I'd like to bring her to you so you can tell her."

I asked Sarah for the child's name and realized that I had met her one morning walking toward our Sunday school classrooms with a friend. She was the quieter of the two girls and looked as if she'd grown awkwardly taller ahead of her peers. She was pale and slightly disheveled. She was the kind of kid you'd notice and grow curious about.

I would soon learn the details. Sarah and the girl were on their way to my office. To this day, it astounds me that a social worker, with years of training and experience, felt it important for the pastor of the girl's only church connection to tell her this bad news. It was as if this tragic news was too much for mere mortals and had to be handled in a sacred space.

I paced the floor for a few minutes and went to the bathroom. I felt nauseous and took a few deep breaths before walking slowly back to the office. My palms grew clammy. I hadn't a clue what to do in this situation.

I let the secretary know that we would need privacy for this very difficult conversation. I filled her in so she wouldn't greet the girl with a funny joke or lighthearted humor as she might have done otherwise. They soon arrived.

This is still one of the hardest memories I have of my years as a local pastor. I was not trauma trained. I leaned on God in a wordless prayer and held that little girl's two small hands in my larger ones as she heard the news that her mother had died. I felt a nearly imperceptible trembling in her hands. I had imagined that she'd scream or cry, but she sat stone still as if she was refusing to hear my words.

The words of Paul came through to me in the sadness at that moment: "Nothing will be able to separate us from the love of God." Not height or depth or even this? Not even when a little girl needs her mother's arms around her and will not have them to lean on from this day on? The scripture passage showed up like a familiar tune you can't shake off and pointed me toward a peace beyond this crazy confusing day when a pastor, a social worker, and a little girl sat with a terrible reality. A day when the sun wouldn't likely break through the fog at all.

> For I am convinced that neither death, nor life, nor angels, nor rulers, nor things present, nor things to come, nor powers, nor height, nor depth, nor anything else in all creation, *will* be able to *separate us from the love of God* in Christ Jesus our Lord.
>
> —Romans 8:38–39

WE WERE all changed that day. The girl's life would be forever redirected. Her new home with her aunt and uncle was charitable, but not warm. Her aunt talked negatively about the child's mother's death. "She messed up all of our lives, that day," she said, oozing resentment. The girl never saw or heard from her father again. And like many trauma survivors she went inside herself to a safer place in the back of her mind and rarely came out. She vowed to never trust in or depend upon another person again. I was later told that she pulled that off until her mid-thirties, when she was blessedly rescued from isolation by a significantly secure relationship. Many trauma survivors fare much worse—ending up in addictive cycles of sex, alcohol, or drugs, suffering chronic physical pain, or using anger and violence to push people as far away as possible.

The day the girl's mother died changed her relationships and behavior. It also changed her neurobiology. The brain adapts to moments of intense fear and that adaptation leaves the brain more vulnerable when future stressors come along. New fields in research are exploring trauma's neurobiology and brain plasticity. The brain's fear centers, the amygdala and hippocampus, are designed to help the emotional system cope with fear, and some studies suggest that they actually change when overloaded, making it harder to cope with subsequent events. The girl experienced a life-changing and brain-changing event.

The social worker and I were changed too. She was motivated to go back to a church she'd been attending and sent me a note of thanks. I saw her next at a local training on suicide prevention. We had both become aware that our education had not provided us with much-needed information about dealing with people in trauma. Years later, while I was in doctoral studies in psychology, I learned that there's a name for all that I thought and felt following this event: It's called secondary traumatic stress. The social worker and I had both walked away from my office that day with more residual trauma than we had words to describe. I can still feel those small hands trembling in my own hands. The experience was seared into the trauma center in my brain. I still carry that little girl in my heart.

Initially after I told the girl about her mother's death, I found myself waking in the night, calling friends more frequently to be sure they were okay, driving on mountain roads more intentionally, and reliving the feeling of her trembling hands in mine. These secondary trauma symptoms are similar to the feelings and behaviors among people who experience trauma firsthand. The initial shock slowly becomes easier to bear. But the traumatic content found its way deep inside me and rested there with reverberations not unlike the shaky hands we once exchanged. Forty years later, I called a colleague up and asked if I could see her to release stored-up trauma from this scene and many others across the span of my pastoral and chaplaincy careers. I'll talk later in the book about this treatment modality and other ways that individuals and care providers can use the brain's neuroplasticity to reduce residual trauma.

When hymn writer Horatio Spafford penned the lyrics to "It Is Well with My Soul," he was processing personal tragedy following multiple traumatic events. His two-year-old son had died in the Great Chicago fire of 1871, his business interests were on shaky ground, and his four daughters had drowned at sea in a shipwreck. He received this news via telegram from his wife, Anna, who had miraculously survived. She simply wrote, "Saved alone. . . ."[1] The hymn's lyrical beauty shines through his pain, and people singing this hymn today are still moved by the hope imbedded in it. When the worst happens, those who find faith and healing remind us that the human spirit is remarkably resilient.

> When peace, like a river, attendeth my way,
> When sorrows like sea billows roll;
> Whatever my lot, Thou hast taught me to say,
> It is well, it is well with my soul.

Peace is one of many surprising feelings that can arise in traumatic circumstances, although sometimes no feelings rise up at all; rather, a sense of numbness and detachment prevails. There isn't a right or a wrong way to process trauma. Every emotional response has a purpose and can lead to greater self-awareness and acceptance. Some survivors draw upon a lifelong faith in God; others experience themselves in a wilderness devoid of spiritual grounding. It may take days, weeks, months, or years to come to grips with an earlier trauma or to work through repeated traumatic experiences.

In this book you will find suggestions that combine psychological treatments with faith resources to improve trauma recovery. If you are a trauma survivor, or a caregiving pastor, church member, or friend to a survivor, this resource is designed to familiarize you with symptoms and healing strategies. It is also an invitation for you to reach out to victims of trauma in ways that are both compassionate and knowledgeable. Research has shown that people in supportive communities can draw upon the strength of others to increase their resiliency. Secure and trusting relationships heal many wounds, and I believe that we are all equipped to hold a small child's hurting hands while her heart breaks. I trust this, even though it is difficult, because God has let me rest my hands in hers.

Part One
Understanding Trauma

1
What Is Trauma?

I was booked on a flight from Oregon to Tucson, Arizona, to lead a church workshop on clergy ethics several years ago. In order for planes from the West Coast to get across the country by the end of the day, our flights typically leave between five and six a.m. I had gotten up in the middle of the night, showered, dressed, and driven to the airport. I sleepwalked through security and waited for the regional jet to begin boarding. It was still dark when I took my seat on the aisle next to a young man in his early thirties who smiled anxiously. He said his name was Bob and that he had booked a window seat because he'd never flown before and he wanted to see the views. Bob was the new manager at a local video game store, and he was heading to Arizona for a regional training event. He was nervously chatting away when the flight attendant gave us the usual instructions. He took out the safety card and reviewed it, an obviously newbie behavior. I took out my noise-canceling headphones.

The plane soon lifted off, heading north and then east, where the sun was breaking over the tops of forested mountains. Streaming orange and pink sunrays cut across the valley—a view so breathtaking that I didn't notice anything amiss. Bob gestured and started to talk, so I lowered my headphones. "Is this how it usually feels on takeoff?" he asked.

The question roused me. And then the plane scooped lower toward the ground and regained altitude on its way up. It swooped again, birdlike. I'd never had an ascent like that one before. My pulse rate rose significantly, but I didn't want to alarm Bob. "It's a little bit sluggish," I said. "Probably nothing."

The captain came over the speaker and said, "Ladies and gentlemen, we are not approaching our target altitude due to a problem with lift." In the bubble over my head I was speaking scary curse words. What the *@#$ is lift? I wondered. It sure sounded important. All the color had drained from Bob's face, which he pressed against the window as if looking down could help. The PA system crackled with the flight attendant's voice this time. "I need to ask you all to keep calm while we give you a few additional safety instructions. The captain is fully able to handle this situation, and he is dropping fuel as we return to the airport." We were barely above a high plateau that is a favorite spot for hikers. I hoped no one was on the trail early.

"Don't we need fuel?" Bob said, starting to panic.

"We will lighten the plane's load, so that we can glide onto the runway," the flight attendant announced, as if she'd heard Bob in our tenth-row seats.

She went on to give us emergency instructions that are not found on the card in the seat pocket. We practiced bracing ourselves for the landing. Being a short person I couldn't put my body into the recommended brace position, but Bob demonstrated that he could. She also told us that we'd be circling around for a while in order to wait for emergency response teams on the ground.

"The plane will be coming in fast," she said. "We will let you know when we are in the approach."

While facing death, everyone I loved popped into my mind. I wondered when I had last told my daughter how much I love her. I considered taking out a marker and writing her a note on the seatback in front of me, but if the plane didn't crash I could be in a lot of trouble. I had recently met with a lawyer to revise my last will and testament. "Thank God for that," I thought. I told myself that I'd had a long-enough life and reviewed my accomplishments. I didn't formulate this into words exactly, but I asked God to please handle this. I was having a hard time distracting myself, and the anxiety kept rising.

I'd spent four years working in the emergency department of a hospital as the weekend chaplain, and I flashed back to some gruesome scenes. This clearly didn't help, so I bargained with God to take me fast rather than burn me up or mangle me in wreckage. And I forced myself to mentally return to my seat and offered Bob a halfhearted smile. He looked worse than I felt.

I asked Bob if we could hold hands on the way down and he said, "Sure," and took my hand right then and there. Then he began his story. "I'm engaged to a wonderful girl and we're going to get married next summer. I've got to get back home in one piece, right?"

"Yes," of course. As a somewhat anxious flyer under normal circumstances, I usually pick out a person on the plane whom I think God would not want to die. I reason that if God spares that other person, then the plane will be safe and I'll be spared too. Over Maui one time in a very small propjet that was bouncing around, I looked at all the passengers and decided that the nun in the back row would save me. This time, it would be Bob and his bride-to-be. It's called magical thinking, I know. I don't believe God works like that. God doesn't spare us or strike us dead on the basis of merit. We are all loved, and we are all vulnerable.

"Well, Bob," I said, gaining a few minutes of increased sanity, "Would you like me to suggest some great places for an outdoor wedding?"

I think he said "okay," but I can't be sure at this point. We both needed something to distract us, so I gave him a California and Oregon travel guide to best wedding venues. I went into details about state and national parks, beautiful waterfalls, places I'd performed wedding ceremonies when I was pastoring churches. It helped us stay calm and future-focused for a little while. It's hard to get emotionally grounded in an airplane that is about to crash-land. But distraction can be temporarily effective.

I was doing alright until I noticed that the pilot was bringing the plane in over a small meandering river. Just in case. No point risking lives on the ground. The flight attendant said we'd soon be in brace position and asked us to secure our things. I glanced around the cabin to see how other people were doing.

The woman behind me was talking to her seatmate about what the "lift" problem meant.

"My husband's a pilot and he's practiced this type of situation," she said. "I'm sure we'll be fine." Between the cracks in our chair backs I could see that she didn't look at all worried. The man across from me had his eyes closed and seemed to be sleeping. It occurred to me that he might have had some powerful anti-anxiety drug with him to help him handle flying and had taken it. Maybe he'd taken two. The couple behind him was holding hands and the wife was crying.

Everyone on the plane responded differently.

"Brace, NOW," the attendant said.

The plane took a light bounce and raced toward the end of the runway. The g-force was so strong that to this day I hate landings; they always seem too fast. The brakes threw us around a bit, but the plane stopped a few yards from the end of the runway. I began sobbing so hard that Bob asked me if I was okay.

"Yes," I said, and kept sobbing huge, grateful tears.

"Wow," said Bob, pointing out the window. We could see two or three ambulances, several fire trucks, the local television truck, and a dozen people in what looked like silver space suits. They were prepared for a crash.

I was suddenly very cold and shaking from my head to my bare toes. I'd worn flip flops that day and later thought this to have been a very stupid choice if I'd needed to run through flames or a broken fuselage. "The next time I board a plane," I promised myself, "I'll wear closed-toed shoes."

Bob stood up, and proclaimed that he would never fly again, "EVER." When the stewardess opened the door he leapt over seats and people to get out. I didn't even get a chance to thank him for holding my hand. Thank you, Bob.

As we deboarded the plane, local television reporters eagerly approached. Despite the fact that I had become a psychologist and the reality that some of my counseling clients would see me on the news, I agreed to make a very brief comment when the microphone was thrust my way.

"Were you scared?" the reporter naïvely asked.

"Absolutely!" I said, looking pale and shivering.

When the pilots and crew came through the crowd, a round of thunderous applause broke out. Later in the day I learned that not one of the crew was willing to get back on that plane.

I had a job to do, so I engaged in a behavioral reset. I went back home and took another shower as if I was starting the day all over again. I ate breakfast. I cuddled the dog. I put on my steel-toed hiking boots and packed the flip flops into my bag. And in a few hours I drove back to the airport and boarded a two o'clock flight as if the whole thing had never happened. As I tell this story even now, my hands are cold, it's hard to get a deep breath, and grateful tears are near the surface. The experience has not fully left my body, nor will it ever.

Threat Perception

Studies have shown that people's perceptions of external threats are lowered when they have a hand to hold. A loved one's hand has the greatest power to lower threats, but even a stranger's hand has the power to calm our fears in dangerous situations.[1]

What Is Trauma?

WE FREQUENTLY hear the word *trauma* used in everyday speech. Someone says, "When my boyfriend broke up with me it was really traumatic." Or "I was traumatized when my boss fired me in front of the whole staff." But do we really know what it means? The English word dates back to the late 1600s. It conveys a sense of psychic wound, hurt, or defeat.

Trauma is much more than an ordinary experience of stress. Each person on the airplane trip with me was threatened with serious harm and possible death. But isn't it amazing that each person responded so differently? After the airplane landed, some of them would call their ordeal traumatic while others would say it was an interesting experience. People who have been shot in a war zone, lived through a horrendous car crash, escaped in the nick of time from a flood or firestorms might read this airplane story and think it's a minor incident. That's precisely why trauma is hard to categorize. So what can we say it typically is?

Trauma is a life-threatening experience that overwhelms our ability to use ordinary cognitive, emotional, and physical coping strategies. We can identify it by symptoms that appear *after* personal or secondary exposure to actual or threatened death, serious injury, or sexual violence. Trauma clearly leaves us changed psychologically, since it affects feelings, thoughts, and behaviors. It lodges itself in our bodies with long-lasting physiological effects, and new studies show that these changes may be transmitted genetically to subsequent generations. It disrupts our spirituality, too. Life-threatening experiences call previously held beliefs into question, and we often come away from them asking deeply spiritual questions about who lives and who dies, God's presence or absence during our toughest life experiences, and what happens to us after we die.

> Trauma is a life-threatening experience that overwhelms our ability to use ordinary cognitive, emotional, and physical coping strategies.

Soul Wound

Psychologist Edwardo Duran, who studies trauma in Native American people and culture, says trauma inflicts a "soul wound." Traumatic experiences due to genocide, war, or racial oppression repeat from one generation to the next.[2] The spiritual pain in successive generations can't be simply explained by psychology or biology. When historical trauma occurs in families, interventions are needed to stop the transmission of soul wounds.

Duran's work affirms the spiritual component of traumatic stress. When trauma occurs, people both rely on and revise their beliefs. Their relationship with God, or other named higher power, shifts dramatically. Making meaning out of trauma is a significant faith journey.

Clinical Definitions

The word "trauma" can refer to a highly stressful single incident or to a cluster of stressors. Repeated traumatic experiences exacerbate our response to any single event. When trauma creates a group of identified psychological symptoms, they are categorized in the Manual of Mental Disorders (DSM-5). Medical providers use these diagnostic labels to formulate treatment plans. Symptoms lasting less than a month are diagnosed as Acute Stress Disorder. Symptoms lasting more than a month are classified as Post Traumatic Stress Disorder (PTSD). Even so-called experts in the field of trauma treatment disagree about trauma's symptoms, duration, and best treatment. They aren't confused; it's just that we all experience and heal very differently from overwhelming stress.

Trauma etches itself into us. I know this personally and from listening to the stories of countless clients who still carry trauma's lingering effects. Clinician, researcher, and pioneer in the field

According to PTSD United, an online support resource, 70 percent of adults in the US have experienced some type of traumatic event at least once in their lives, and 20 percent of these people go on to develop PTSD. That equates roughly to 44.7 million people who were or are struggling with PTSD.[3]

of traumatic stress Bessel van der Kolk[4] offers another working definition of trauma. When interviewed by *Psychotherapy Networker*, he described trauma as *an event that overwhelms the central nervous system*. Trauma is a whole-body physiological response. It affects the brain by altering memory, emotion, and cognition. It changes the way that people process and recall memories. As van der Kolk notes, "Trauma is not the story of something that happened back then. . . . It's the current imprint of that pain, horror, and fear living inside people."[5]

From childhood through adolescence and adulthood we accumulate trauma. If we grow up in an abusive family or endure sexual abuse, we become especially vulnerable to subsequent stressors. If we grow up in poverty we are even more likely to experience multiple traumatic incidents during childhood. If we are assaulted, abused, or left homeless at an early age, we have to cope with and use skills that aren't usually needed until adulthood. Parental divorce also leaves us vulnerable to later complicated stress.

In adolescence we lack the ability to accurately perceive risk while simultaneously engaging in risk-taking behaviors, increasing our exposure to potentially traumatic events. Maybe we drive too fast or take a ride with someone who is drunk or hitchhike. We may party with drugs or binge drink for the first time or move into a culture of substance abuse and violence. Because we take more risks, we may even experience a friend's death or come close to death ourselves.

Entering college or early work life exposes us to different risks. Sexual exploration can lead to unprotected hookups, coercion, and exploitation. Date rape is all too common. Researchers estimate that between 30 and 60 percent of women are victims of rape or attempted rape before the age of twenty-five.[6] Men are also sexually assaulted, though they less frequently report their experiences. Sexual encounters involving intense fear are tragically commonplace.

> Trauma etches itself into us.

By our middle years, many of us will have stood at a grave after the sudden tragic death of a family member or friend. Some of us will have experienced intimate partner violence. Too many of us will have been terrified by threatened or actual gun violence or know someone who has been through this devastating trauma. In our older years, when we take time for life review, we don't often stop to tally up our accumulated traumatic incidents. Yet, they may still be affecting our overall well-being.

As you read through this book you may find yourself recalling fearful experiences you hadn't previously defined as "traumatic."

Trauma's Far-Reaching Impact

Cultural factors increase the likelihood that trauma will have a lasting impact. Some studies suggest that Hispanic Americans are at greater risk for developing PTSD than other cultural groups. African American and Hispanic American war veterans have been found to have higher rates of PTSD among all US enlisted personnel.[7] Ongoing study is needed to understand these cultural differences.

People of all ethnicities experience stress due to unemployment and poverty. Consider the anxiety-inducing immigrant's journey—including days without food, fearing for children's safety, risking one's life to cross a border—all the while fearing family separation. In the United States, the double stigma of immigration and racial prejudice too often impede successful trauma recovery. Multicultural studies continue to explore variations in trauma responses based on social, economic, and ethnic characteristics.

People who have served in military combat zones have seen multiple horrific incidents of death and dismemberment. They have lived with constant fear for their own lives. Military personnel who have not been deployed into violent situations are still frequently exposed to the traumatic stories of their peers. They experience personal trauma and secondary (also called tertiary) trauma. And their trauma is transferred to their loved ones.

A soldier who returned from Iraq came to our small town to live with his parents while he recovered from his combat deployment. His mother, Julie, was troubled by his behavior, and after many sleepless nights she called me. I was the pastor of their church, and even though I had not met Oscar, I was honored to hear about him.

"Oscar has totally changed since his last tour of duty," Julie said. "He numbs himself out in front of the computer or television, he never laughs like he used to. He gets a blank stare on his face a lot, and says he needs to drink to 'stop remembering.'" Julie went on to say that thanks to a generous employer, Oscar had gotten a job pumping gas at the local Shell station. One evening at work, a truck backfired in the parking lot. Instantly terrified, Oscar went inside the office and sat in the corner shaking while customers outside grew angry. He didn't translate the sound accurately and think, "It's just a truck backfiring." To him it was gunfire, and he had to run for his life.

Listening to the story, I recognized Oscar's traumatic symptoms. Oscar's heart rate had soared as his adrenal system instantly took charge of his body and prepared him to flee, fight, or freeze. His frontal cortex, the region of the brain responsible for thought and discretion, had shut down within seconds after the noise. He was on autopilot, without the ability to control his responses.

Oscar told his mother that evening, "I couldn't think, I just had to crawl to safety. When my boss found me like that, he said he was sorry but he had to fire me."

Julie was understandably concerned about her son's deterioration. It was time for prayer and an intervention. I called the local Veteran's

> "Throughout evolution humans have been exposed to terrible events; yet most people who are exposed to dreadful experiences survive without developing psychiatric disorders. Throughout history, some people have adapted to terrible life events with flexibility and creativity, while others have become fixated on the trauma and gone on to lead traumatized and traumatizing existences."
> — Bessel Van der Kolk, *Traumatic Stress*[8]

Administration office and found a support group, which Julie thought she could convince Oscar to attend. I provided Julie with the names of local counselors so that she could see someone too and learn to lower her own stress while helping Oscar.

Trauma Defined by War

In the 1940s, just after WWII ended, psychiatrists began studying war trauma among veterans. As a young psychologist my father was deployed to help wounded soldiers in recovery from what they called "shell shock." He kept a journal in which he noted the misery these men suffered and his feelings of powerlessness to treat them. Early psychiatric medications often had terrible side effects and were not effective in treating symptoms. Those who worked in war hospitals also had secondary PTSD though they did not know what to call it. My father said that he "didn't have the constitution" for the work and became sullen and depressed.

The post-WWII era provided psychiatric researchers with the opportunity to study the difference between those who improved and those who did not. Some soldiers overcame their nervousness and depression through the compassion of those who came to their bedsides. When families were reunited, many patients found strength and resilience as they returned home and were honored in their communities. A few, sadly, were so dissociated, they needed lifelong psychiatric care.

What was the difference between those who came home unscathed and those who had lingering post-traumatic stress symptoms? By studying "shell shock" (a term no longer used), psychiatrists observed and categorized symptoms such as changes in mood and cognition, including hypervigilance, sleep disturbances, flashbacks, and distressing memories. They studied physiological changes, including appetite loss and gastrointestinal distress. And they studied behaviors such as social withdrawal and avoidance of situations that might evoke triggering stimuli. Once they categorized symptoms,

> He was on autopilot, without the ability to control his responses.

the American Psychiatric Association (APA) began to formulate a diagnosis they called Post Traumatic Stress Disorder (PTSD).

This classification scheme stipulated that the traumatic event was something beyond an individual's control. Lifting the shame from the disorder went a long way toward cultural acceptance of this mental illness. Soldiers could be treated for a documentable problem rather than condemned for their lack courage or bravery. Once the symptoms were clearly identified and measured consistently across many types of traumatic experiences, patients began telling stories about various painful and fearful events and getting help to heal the aftermath of trauma.

By the 1980s, the Diagnostic and Statistical Manual of the American Psychiatric Association (DSM-III) had broadened the definition of PTSD to include events such as war, torture, rape, and imprisonment. Survivors of natural disasters such as floods, fires, earthquakes, and other life-threatening circumstances could be diagnosed with PTSD.

A woman who was held at gunpoint when a robber invaded her home was given the diagnosis, along with a man who had been raped in prison. A teenager who survived a train crash in which his sister died received the diagnosis.

More common circumstances such as bereavement or being fired at work are now given the Adjustment Disorder diagnosis. The original shapers of the PTSD diagnosis had discovered that recovery from traumatic events was clearly different from the healing process that took place after painful stressors that constitute the normal vicissitudes of life such as divorce, failure, rejection, serious illness, financial reverses, and the like.[9] They expected that these lesser stressors could be overcome in three to six months. When symptoms prevail for a long while, different interventions are needed and beneficial. A trauma diagnosis provides survivors with a better understanding of symptoms, a roadmap for recovery, and the financial resource of medical insurance to treat enduring symptoms.

Over the years since the initial categories for PTSD were chosen, they have been challenged in treatment and in court. Since trauma results from so many different circumstances and is experienced so differently, a categorical approach may not be advisable. Some psychiatrists argue that looking at a range of symptoms and measuring their intensity would be a more accurate way to determine the diagnosis. Diverse human experiences, including culture, religion, ethnicity, and gender, are all variables in a person's response to trauma. Practitioners consider multiple factors when establishing the diagnosis. They examine both the event that overwhelms the nervous system and the environment in which the trauma and recovery take place.

Studies in Trauma Resilience

People who get through dreadful experiences and survive them with minimal symptoms are being studied for their resilience. What makes us resilient or not? Van der Kolk suggests that the ability to integrate the trauma is what makes the difference. After a traumatic experience integration involves finding new language for our internal experience, rewriting our history. It also means learning from the experience, reflecting upon spiritual meaning and values, and thinking about ourselves and others differently.

If you went to a therapist after a traumatic event, the therapist might ask you the following questions in order to help you with the process of integration.

- How do you make sense out of what happened to you?
- In what ways did it make you stronger or more vulnerable?
- How can you offer yourself compassion for how you handled the experience or its aftermath?
- What have you learned about yourself in your healing journey?

Trauma survivors are most resilient when they are supported by others who listen without judgment and validate them. Going to a therapist is one way to receive unconditional regard. Victims

> Trauma survivors are most resilient when they are supported by others who listen without judgment and validate them.

who seek out nonshaming support people can learn that they are not crazy even while feeling so. Turning to a close friend, a compassionate pastor, or a support group can also help.

When people live in what van der Kolk calls "an unprotected" environment and have to fend for themselves, the outcome is very different. Families and congregations are key sources of strength and resilience for trauma survivors. A congregation can provide vital relationships for those who are on the road to trauma resilience.

Overlapping Traumatic Incidents

Television reporters interviewed two bank tellers who had been held at gunpoint during a bank robbery. The police apprehended the suspects later in the day, and no one had been physically injured. Both women told a similar story about the robbery, but the first one began to shake and get weepy as she talked. The second one was almost blasé by comparison. "It was just another day, another experience," she said. Why the difference? The first woman had previously been through a life-threatening bank robbery in which she and a coworker locked themselves in the safe deposit vault, uncertain what they would find when they came out. That single variable left her more vulnerable to an acute trauma response.

The US Department of Veterans Affairs notes, "Trauma, like pain, is not an external phenomenon that can be completely objectified. Like pain, the traumatic experience is filtered through cognitive and emotional processes before it can be appraised as an extreme threat." We all have different ways to appraise the threats we experience. "Different people appear to have different trauma thresholds, some more protected from and some more vulnerable to developing clinical symptoms after exposure to extremely stressful situations."[10]

Each person on the airplane with Bob and me when the lift system failed had the same experience, but we didn't come away with the same trauma. One of the flight attendants sat next to me on my subsequent flight to Tucson. She was still shaken up. Would this cause her to consider a career change? Did my seatmate Bob keep his pledge to never board a plane again, or did he eventually get back on an airplane and take his fiancée on a honeymoon? Without knowing the backstories in the lives of each passenger, I couldn't tell you how the threat impacted them or their chances of fully putting it behind them. Nor could I predict their future behaviors without analyzing their emotional resilience and level of interpersonal support, nor without exploring what that morning meant to them.

When a woman I'll call Sarah came to my counseling office, she told me that she had been assaulted and nearly raped in a field where she was walking her dog. She fought off her attacker and made it home with minor bruises. Over the next few days she slept poorly, felt nauseous, and barely ate. Her moods ranged from anger to sadness, and she felt constantly irritable with her husband. I wondered about her history and what earlier life experiences could be influencing her recovery. Over months in treatment, trust grew slowly between us, and eventually she was able to tell me the whole story. Sarah was vulnerable to PTSD because her older brother had sexually abused her beginning when she was five years old and into her teenage years. As an adult she had repressed these memories. For nearly sixty years, until the day in the field when she was grabbed from behind, she went about life as if nothing bad had happened to her. But that night in the field it all came back to her.

Fighting the assailant off, she experienced for the first time that she could keep herself safe during an assault. As a young girl, she never could. In her recovery process, we had to go back to her earlier trauma, to help her reduce the pain she'd been avoiding for years, but we didn't stay there long. We affirmed the strength she had developed across her lifespan to keep herself safe. This strength gave her what she needed to remain mindful in the present day and avoid being emotionally pulled back into memories and feelings from her terrifying childhood abuse. Sarah came to understand her vulnerability to traumatic stress as a normal response and accept it without judgment.

Initial Biological Responses

When traumatic incidents occur, our bodies are prepared to respond. As is written in Psalm 139, we are "fearfully and wonderfully made." Fear is a physical response. Perspiration, quickened breathing, rapid heart rate, reduced circulation, and nausea all normally occur in high-stress situations. The body is designed to shut down unnecessary functions, such as thinking and digesting food, when it needs all of its resources for survival. We have called this the "fight or flight" syndrome, but it is now known that freezing is another common response, especially for women. The body consolidates energy in order to fight, flee, or freeze.

During and immediately after trauma, while the brain helps us out, three cognitive dissociative disorders typically occur. According to the American Psychiatric Association, "Dissociative disorders involve problems with memory, identity, emotion, perception, behavior and sense of self. Dissociative symptoms can potentially disrupt every area of mental functioning."[11] They include dissociative amnesia, dissociative identity disorder, and depersonalization/derealization disorder.

Dissociative amnesia cleverly protects us by limiting our psychological/emotional awareness and keeping horrifying experiences out of sight. We simply can't remember details that would be too painful to recall. With dissociative identity disorder (formerly called multiple personality disorder) flexible personality structures in our brains adapt to trauma by forming multiple selves to withstand and combat the onslaught of trauma and fear. With depersonalization disorder, our core self is numb to the rest of the

> We simply can't remember details that would be too painful to recall.

Every year during cold season I get a flu shot, but it doesn't always work. When I catch a cold or get the flu it goes into my chest, which I attribute to childhood asthma and growing up in a household of smokers. I have more vulnerability to bronchitis. In a similar way, trauma victims are more likely than others to feel powerless in moments that include unwanted and uncomfortable symptoms. There is no shame in this. It's just vulnerability.

world and cut off from other people. When we are victimized we turn inward, the way a snail pulls into its shell or a starfish recoils under the touch of a dangerous predator. This withdrawal can help us to avoid further exposure at a highly sensitive time. Sometimes the withdrawal results in numbness to feelings. This too is adaptive. It helps us block out overwhelming emotions and avoid paralyzing horror. When derealization disorder occurs, we walk ghostlike through life as in a dream to protect ourselves and others from the realities that accompanied the dreadful experience.

Our brains are perfectly designed to protect us at times of stress and arousal. The hypothalamus activates the stress response. First the autonomic nervous system (ANS) sends its messages through clusters of nerve fibers to the central nervous system, which telegraphs the news to the body, saying, "Take action for safety's sake." The ANS controls the involuntary activity in the body and excites the sympathetic nervous system (SNS), which increases our heart rate, dilates our pupils, inhibits salivation, relaxes our lungs, circulates glucose, and even releases the contents in our bladders. Like an early warning system, the SNS readies us for response. When nerves stimulate our adrenal glands, we are flooded with hormones known as neurotransmitters, including epinephrine and norepinephrine. These functions make us strong runners and quick responders when danger lurks.

At a continuing education training, I learned about a recently developed method of cognitive therapy called ACT (Action and Commitment Therapy).[12] The trainer described the genetic benefits of our body's quick-acting response, illustrating with a story about two rabbits lying in the grass. The rabbits are munching happily away, when they suddenly see a fox approaching. The first rabbit stops to think about the fox: "I wonder what the fox had to eat last night" or "Maybe the fox isn't hungry, just passing by." While he contemplates his situation and sizes up his best escape plan, he stands in the path of the fox too long, and the fox grabs and eats him. The second rabbit simply runs to a hole in the ground as fast as his legs can take him. He safely reaches his hiding place. And while he can feel the fox's breath descending from the hole above, the fox cannot get to him. This reinforces the second rabbit's physiological tendencies to shut off his brain and run like heck. The second rabbit lives on and reproduces, so his offspring become safety-action oriented as well. This increases their survival rates. In a similar way, humans have genetically evolved to experience fear in order to improve our survival rate.

Human brains have an even greater capacity than the rabbit's brain. Our brains photograph dangerous scenes during traumatic events. During trauma, our fearful experiences are lodged in our right brains like collages and jumbled-up, dream-like images. But since the hippocampus shuts down during trauma, it cannot pass material from the right brain (mental pictures are stored there) to the left brain, where linear thought and story lines make "sense" out of nonsensical experiences. Instead, these picture memories appear again later, and they are called flashbacks. When flashbacks occur, our mind is not trying to retraumatize us. Rather, the mind is trying to move undifferentiated images that were seared into our brains at the time of the fearful experience into long-term memory to release their hold on our psyches.

After the sympathetic nervous system goes to work to help us respond in the presence of fear, another helpful system—a group of nervous system fibers called the parasympathetic nervous system—emerges. These return the body to homeostasis. They slow the heart rate and lower the blood pressure after the sympathetic nervous system has activated the fight or flight response. My sobbing tears after our airplane landed safety were initiated by my parasympathetic nervous system to help my body release the overload of adrenaline I'd been carrying.

There are ways to increase the power and effectiveness in the parasympathetic response system. I used some strategies to lower my trauma at the time of my close call with a plane crash and afterward. I shared the experience with Bob, and I held his hand, which lowered the threat level in my body. I was able to use meditation techniques to tune into my body and consciously slow my breath and pulse rate. I used the experience to learn how to better protect myself in the future (I have not worn open-toed shoes on an airplane since). To get back on another plane that day, I went home and used my imagination and raw courage in order to start the day over.

At the workshop the morning after my harrowing flight to Tucson, I knew I was off my game. I felt physically exhausted, as if I'd run the New York City Marathon the day before. I briefly told workshop participants what had happened, so I could lower my perfectionistic expectations for the day. I found that telling this story also connected me to people in the room, who were instantly drawn into the experience. Many of them had also had near crashes by car, truck, or plane. At that moment we were all connected through God's grace and great gratitude to be alive that day. We didn't sing the song, but I had the melody running through my head all day long. "And are we yet alive, and see each other's face? Glory and thanks to Jesus give for his almighty grace!"[13]

What You'll Be Learning

In subsequent chapters I'll explore trauma's effects on the body, brain, spirituality, identity, and relationships. This book includes insights for caregivers—family members, friends, clergy, or congregationally trained lay ministers—who play a critical role in the life of those who have been traumatized. A survivor's trust in others and the world is so often shattered by trauma. Trustworthy people restore the survivor's faith in humanity and help survivors reconnect to themselves and others. A psychology professor, Philip A. Fisher at the University of Oregon, has researched "super survivors," people who bounce back and even grow after trauma. He has found that "the people who survive and rebound from trauma frequently had an early caregiver who pumped unshakable love into them, and that built a rock of inner security they could stand on for the rest of their lives."[14] It's never too late for victims to find that inner security.

> Questions for personal reflection and small-group discussions are included at the end of each chapter throughout the book. If you are participating in a group or are a group leader, please note that talking about trauma is sometimes very powerful and can also be emotionally overwhelming. Make sure no one in your group feels pressured to answer any question, and perhaps let your participants pick the question they want to respond to. As you will learn later in the book, talking about trauma too soon or under pressure is retraumatizing. Letting people voluntarily tell stories when they are ready to tell them can lead to hope and healing. Be gentle with yourself and with your group as you review the material in the book and respond to these questions.

Unfortunately, in far too many circumstances the survivor's family is the place of wounding and/or can't provide a safe emotional space in which to recover. When that is true, skillful clergy and therapists need to step in to repair the damage. Throughout the book, I will provide useful tools to help caregivers and victims find and define what Fisher called the "rock of inner security."

I recall the story of a young boy who was frightened during a storm. His mother went to his room and stood at his bedside, patted his back, and helped him to calm down. She returned to bed, but another lightning bolt and thunder crack disturbed the boy again. She went to his bedside and held his hand. "There, there," she said, "it'll be all right. God is right here with us looking over us."

"I know," the boy said, sounding more frustrated than ever, "but I want someone with skin on."

Whether you are a victim or a care provider, you can be God's skin-on for others. Victims who have come through devastation are often the *most powerful* healers.

The last sections in this book provide concrete ways that victims address and heal trauma. If you are a trauma victim, you will likely find a version of your own story here as I share the voices of others. Each person's name and identifying information has been disguised to protect their right to own their own stories, but their stories carry universal truths. I thank them for teaching me the process of recovery as we worked together in my clinical practice, classroom,

> Victims who have come through devastation are often the *most powerful* healers.

parish ministry, and hospital chaplaincy. It is my hope that victims will find similarities to their own stories here and recognize that they are not alone or "crazy." There are as many ways to define recovery as there are to define trauma, and we all experience healing uniquely. Perhaps the information you read here will move you forward in hope. There's a very good chance that full recovery is possible for you or for someone you know and love.

For Reflection and Discussion

1 Describe an experience that overwhelmed your ability to use your typical coping strategies.

2 Talk about a generational soul wound in your extended family.

3 In what ways might you be vulnerable (or not vulnerable) to traumatic stress?

4 How is your faith community serving traumatized people?

5 Who are the people in your life who have "pumped unshakable love" into you?

2
Trauma's Aftermath

ONE HUNDRED fifty beats per minute. I checked my pulse rate when I finished telling psychology students in the university class I was teaching about my airplane incident. My heart was beating about twice as fast as usual, even though more than ten years had passed since the day my plane nearly crashed. How was that possible? In this chapter we will be looking at some of the physical, cognitive, emotional, and behavioral symptoms that typically follow trauma. These symptoms can appear hours, days, months, or years after the traumatic event.[1]

My church office secretary phoned me on my day off and apologized but continued, "I think you'll want to know this."

I let out a long sigh. "Okay, what's going on?"

"Naomi's mom just called, because Naomi's in the psych ward at the hospital. She found her boyfriend dead early this morning in their garage." She stopped to take a breath before saying, "He hanged himself."

"I can't imagine anything worse than finding him like that," I said.

I wondered if my secretary was like millions of people who have lost a family member to suicide. If so, she would have been triggered by this phone call. I put it in my thoughts to ask her as soon as possible.

"I'll go see her at the hospital right away."

While driving twenty minutes, parking my car, and walking through several hospital corridors, I had a little time to think. What I first came up with was self-doubt. I had to push back an internal verbal barrage from my superego suggesting that I was untrained for this task and would likely say something "really stupid."

"I'll do what I can," I told myself. "And I'll listen."

Standing before oversized locked double doors, I reached to the side and buzzed the nursing station for permission to enter. The nurse who answered knew me and let me in. I heard the lock clunk and went through the slowly opening entry doors on autopilot. My mind was telling me to "run," "go back," "get out now while you can." My psyche was alerted to vicarious trauma's dangerousness.

The nurse ushered me into Naomi's room. Naomi was sitting on a hospital bed near the back wall with her knees tucked up under her chin. Her long black hair was draped over her face and fell over her crossed arms. When she lifted her head and saw me, it seemed as if she was a mile away. Her gaze was blank, her eyes red. I asked for permission to pull up a desk chair and sit a few feet away. She nodded yes and reached for my hand, as a child would who was learning to walk, grasping at something nearby to keep from falling. I was praying like crazy. As writer Anne Lamott says, sometimes "Help!" is a powerful prayer. I also called up the 23rd Psalm, "Yea, though I walk through the valley of the shadow of death, I will fear no evil." Her clammy hand was trembling, and I let her leave it in mine and then take it back at her own pace.

"I'm so sorry," I said. And I kept silent yet again.

Eventually she turned toward me on the bed.

"I didn't know," she said weakly. "He didn't leave a note for me—nothing at all."

I shook my head and sighed.

"So here I am in the hospital, living with a bunch of really crazy people and feeling like I belong here, you know?"

I nodded.

"Would it help to talk about it?" I asked. I wanted her to set the pace.

"When anyone else cries on the ward, I cry too," she said. "Isn't that amazing?"

"Babies do that in the intensive care nursery too," I offered.

"Well, I can't stop crying." And tears flowed.

I didn't give her tissues or reassuring words, though I wanted to do something. Any action or verbiage on my part would have disrupted her. She needed me to witness her body gripped with pain. I knew it would be hard to come alongside her in this way, and that's why I had wanted to turn back at the entryway.

"Anyone slams a door," she said, "and I can hear my own door to the house slam behind me. I can see him there . . ." Her voice trailed off as she relived the moment. Her breathing sped up and her hands shook. I said her name firmly.

"Naomi."

I knew intuitively to call her back into the present moment. This is a technique I'd learn later and often use with counseling clients. As her pastor, I didn't need a tool bag. I needed compassion—which means quite literally the ability to suffer with her.

I asked her if I could offer a prayer and she nodded yes. I prayed that her suffering be relieved over time, and I prayed for staff members who would be helping her through it. I thanked God for understanding the tremendous pain her boyfriend had been silently experiencing. I thanked God for warmly receiving him into the life beyond this one. I left space at the end of my prayer in case she had words to add, but the silence continued until I offered the "amen."

> I didn't need a tool bag. I needed compassion—which means quite literally the ability to suffer with her.

I told Naomi to call me at any time when she felt lonely or overwhelmed. And I took a deliberately slow walk down the hall, back through the locked doors, and out to my car.

Naomi met with the staff psychiatrist every day during her hospital stay; because she felt she couldn't go on living if that picture in her head didn't go away. She'd been told once that if she left her computer on without a screensaver, the pixels would burn through the screen."That's what happened in your brain," the psychiatrist told her. "You've got to give it time and rest to make the adjustment."

When a love-bond is suddenly severed, our bodies experience sharp pain.

Naomi didn't need scientific evidence; she felt a greater pain than any she had ever experienced. Her psychiatrist helped her through the worst days with medication, the way she'd have been helped if her pain had been caused by major surgery. The psychiatrist also helped her to visualize good days they had experienced and to use an imaginary "clicker" to change the scene on her internal PowerPoint screen. "Click" away the garage scene, and "click" on their walk by the ocean.

In a few weeks she made a return-to-home plan. The plan included having someone stay at the house with her for a while. She drew upon her faith to picture her boyfriend curled up in the lap of Mary, the mother of Jesus. She pictured Mary reaching down and tenderly wiping away his tears. She wrote letters to him every day. She expressed her many emotions with friends and family who provided empathy and support. She talked to the staff chaplain at

> Helen Fisher, PhD, is an anthropologist specializing in love. In a popular TED Talk she describes the way that the brain sends pain signals through the body when love is lost. She cites a study in which people who have broken up with lovers were placed in scanning machines that track brain activity. When they were shown pictures of their ex- partner, the part of their brain that lit up was the physical pain center. The same place that lights up when a bone breaks or a migraine happens. Losing love hurts.[2]

the hospital and learned to let go of the "whys" in her mind that got her nowhere. She prepared to see a therapist each week and to go to a suicide survivor group.

Commonly Experienced Symptoms

What common symptoms might Naomi experience in the weeks following her hospital stay? Many people with trauma just don't know what to expect afterward. The list of possible symptoms can be overwhelming, especially for someone like Naomi, who felt so disoriented.

Physical and psychological symptoms begin immediately or soon after a traumatic event. An emergency room doctor started feeling physical distress while he bandaged a man's badly mangled body following a helicopter crash. When a colleague inquired about the case, he struggled to recall the order in which he provided the treatments. A college student who was date raped at a party on campus experienced flashbacks a few days later when she had to report the incident to the police. An army medic's trauma symptoms began months later when she returned to the safety of her parents' home. Her inability to tell her parents about all that she had seen left her feeling "stupid" and isolated.

All of these trauma survivors experienced common distressing symptoms. While not all of them fully met the criteria list for PTSD as categorized in the DSM-5,[3] they all experienced one or more very disturbing symptoms. In this chapter we explore traumatic memory disruptions—including amnesia, dissociation, and intrusive memories. In the next chapter we will look at mood and behavior disruptions. I will also revisit these symptoms along with concrete healing strategies in chapters ahead.

Repeated and Upsetting Dreams

First, here's a little brain science. Our dorsal vagal nervous system, a primitive system common to all animals, kicks in when our life is threatened or we feel like it is. Normally, the dorsal vagus, a nerve at the back of the brain (or hindbrain), serves a very positive function. It regulates the body throughout the day as circumstances cause us to fluctuate between arousal and relaxation. In moments when we become too aroused, the dorsal vagus nerve can shut down the entire system and we go into freeze. Suddenly we are immobilized, much like the deer-in-the-headlights phenomenon.

Overwhelming fear disrupts memory processing. This disruption leads to repeated and upsetting dreams, flashbacks, and distress during exposure to trauma-like cues. What happens when memories that are disrupted during trauma become disruptive themselves afterward?

Tanvi's freshman year at the University of California in Berkeley was marked by loneliness and solitude. She and her family had recently moved to California from India, so her father could teach at the university. Fitting into her new surroundings was daunting, but she decided to follow the lead of her peers and attended parties where binge drinking was the norm. At a fraternity event, someone dropped a date-rape drug in her first and only drink. She was targeted by a man who led her to a private room. Her agreement to kiss him was the only consent he asked for or that she gave. He took it to mean that he could do more. She awakened hours later to discover that she had been raped.

Tanvi numbly walked through her next few days with help from the rape assault team on campus. She filed a police report, though she had little recall of the event and couldn't provide many details. Since her body's trauma response and the drug disrupted her ability to make conscious memories, reporting was a frustrating experience.

After her initial shock wore off, she began having disturbing dreams. The memories that she couldn't consciously access were there in her dream world, where they were vividly horrifying. At first she dreamt that she could see the man who raped her on top of her, but he was faceless, and she wasn't even sure the feet she saw in the dream were her feet. She also experienced a repeated dream that he was around a corner on campus, ready to grab her. After a terrifying night when she

> Overwhelming fear disrupts memory processing.

dreamt that he was chasing her across campus, she started avoiding going to bed at night. This disrupted her mental health and her ability to remain in school.

What could possibly help Tanvi with her dreams? Tanvi went to the campus health center to see a physician's assistant. She was prescribed a medication for sleep. She didn't want to take it, so she signed up for therapy at the nurse's insistence. Her counselor, Moriah, helped her to further understand her symptoms.

"Tanvi, your psyche knows that you've been through a very frightening experience, and these dreams are trying to help you resolve the emotional load you carry."

"Help?" Tanvi was incredulous. "I'm afraid to go to bed at night; I leave all the lights on, which bothers my roommate. I lock the door to my room and then check it again—several times."

"Yes, you are on high alert."

"But what about these terrible dreams?"

"Your dream world is presenting you with memories, so you can process them at night. The mind is moving your memories from your right brain, where they are all a jumble of pictures and feelings, into your left brain, where they can organize themselves into stories that help you to make sense of the world. Your dreams help you to cope with your terrors overnight when you can tolerate them because you are in a more relaxed state.

"It's hard enough in the daytime, and now it's wrecking my nights."

"There's also the possibility that these dreams are rehearsals. You imagine a man stepping out into your path, and your dream helps you plan what to do and act on that plan. What would you do, say, if your rapist was chasing you down the street? Does he catch you? Or does something intervene and you get away?"

"I wake up before anything terrible happens."

"Well, that's a good thing, right?"

Tanvi smiled for the first time in a long while.

In therapy, Tanvi learned to trust that these dreams were a sign that her mind was actually finishing something, rather than harming her. Moriah taught her to re-create the dreams with her own endings—she gets free, she turns and screams, or the police grab her assailant.

Tanvi found ways to go to sleep in a less anxious state. She used progressive relaxation in the evening before going to bed. She tensed and released each muscle group in her body and felt each area relax. She listened to soothing music at bedtime. Using these various techniques, she felt more hopeful about getting to sleep easily and staying asleep throughout the night. If these techniques didn't work or she fell back into terror at night, she said she would fill her prescription for sleep medication and try it for a few weeks to reset her disrupted sleep-wake cycle. By conceptualizing her experience in a positive way, Tanvi became less distressed by her trauma-reenacting dreams. Deep in the night, neuropathways in her brain cleared away her traumatic wounds and produced hormones that could flood her again with a sense of well-being and calm.

Flashbacks

A flashback is a sudden and vivid memory from the past that intrudes into the present in such a way that the trauma appears to be occurring in the here and now. It is a vivid mental recall of an earlier event. Flashbacks can be triggered by similar experiences, sudden noises, being startled, or overhearing news about a similar situation. In the aftermath of a school shooting a student remarked that every bell at the end of a class period sounded like a gunshot. The memory intrudes, either in whole or in part. Victims feel themselves helplessly thrown back in time—unwittingly transported back to the original circumstance and trauma.

How are flashbacks formed? When fear and adrenaline race through the body, long-lasting changes take place in the brain. Message-processing centers in the brain get overwhelmed and shut down, so the body picks up the task of holding feelings and memories.

In the primitive center of the brain's temporal lobe where sensory information is gathered and processed, the amygdala (the area responsible for emotions and survival instincts) is alert for environmental dangers. It sends messages to the hippocampus, which has primary responsibility for long-term memory, and connects the right and left hemispheres. The hippocampus serves as a bridge across which memories move from the right to the left brain. But when both of these areas go into panic mode and are overwhelmed, communication between them breaks down. The amygdala grows larger, leaving the survivor with higher levels of anxiety.

In an admittedly simplified way, we could say that the amygdala raises a drawbridge and memories can't cross over to the hippocampus. The memory system can fully shut down and leave a survivor with full or partial amnesia. A common example of this takes place when a person is in a car skidding on the ice and later can't recall the few moments before coming to a stop on the side of the road.

The memory system fails when the brain is under so much stress that it stops shaping and storing memories. The mental bridge that helps us make sense of things is washed out. Traumatic memories get stored in the right brain, where they are pictures and undifferentiated emotions. They become lodged in a chaotic, nonlinear fashion. Flashbacks and nightmares are images that pop up in a montage of scenes and emotions. When the hippocampus is calmly working again, memories can move across the bridge and into the left brain, where we begin to make sense of what happened to us.

The brain has a complicated and adaptive survival plan. Physical responses to trauma are not about personality, faith, or a lack of faith. Overwhelming and even chaotic anxiety is not a sign of weakness. It's an emergency response system—like a firefighter rushing to put out a fire—part of the body's intricate way to keep us alive. The brain adapts itself to assist us, building in these failsafe systems, which can initially seem problematic but help us by making us aware that we are reaching the limits of our capacity to tolerate stress.

Sue was sideswiped on a highway in her town that was known for being particularly dangerous. When an SUV ran a red light, she swerved off the road to avoid it and crashed into a parked car. She went through a year of physical therapy to restore her injured neck and then a year with lawyers and litigation in order to be fairly compensated. Having to repeatedly tell her story and feeling like a pawn in the legal system added to her feeling of hopelessness. But vivid memories disturbed her even more.

Sue frequently experienced flashbacks at night and during the day. She'd be at her work desk and then suddenly be back at the accident scene and see the truck sliding into her. She'd be lying on the couch one minute watching television and then, as if the channel had changed, she'd be in the ambulance again lying on a back brace on the way to the hospital. These vivid sensations included screeching sounds, sirens, and the crunch of her car door buckling. A flashback is disturbing precisely because it is a very vividly detailed sensory memory.

What was going on in Sue's brain? Since the hippocampus in Sue's brain was overwhelmed by the surging fear she felt at the time of the accident, it shut down, and her memories were stored as picture and feeling fragments in her right brain. The flashbacks were her body's way of transferring undifferentiated picture memories from her right brain into her left brain, where she could have better control over her emotional symptoms.

Sue eventually managed to quiet down the flashbacks. How? She learned to reduce the size of pictures she had on her visual screen. When she "saw" the full scene before her, she reduced it to the size of a postage stamp. She then placed an alternative picture in her visual screen overlaid with the word "relax," and then said the

> A flashback is disturbing precisely because it is a very vividly detailed sensory memory.

word aloud. Using these techniques, her flashbacks became more manageable. She gained control and felt less anxiety.

Dissociated Memories

During flashbacks, a trauma victim has awareness of both the past and the present moment. The present mind can address the intruding past, as illustrated in the way that Sue, during a flashback, could "see" a car coming toward her about to crash and simultaneously clear that picture from her mind.

As explained in chapter one, during complex trauma, dissociation involves a disruption in memory, awareness, and perception. The brain can totally block out some or part of the traumatic experience. Dissociation can be adaptive at the time of trauma by helping us get through an overwhelming terror. Later, it keeps us from reexperiencing that same terror. Dissociated physical sensation, memory, and emotions keep trauma survivors alive and help them cope in the recovery process. But those very same strategies can become maladaptive.

For example, extreme abuse at a young age can lead to dissociative identity disorder. It is believed that when abuse occurs before the personality is fully shaped, people have the mental capacity to split into parts. This splitting serves to keep some aspects of the vulnerable self away from traumatic memories. This rare but clinically proven condition can keep victims isolated and numb for many years.

While sitting together at a group therapy session, childhood abuse survivors talked about their adult lives as they coped with multiple personalities. These survivors described themselves as many different people in one body and frequently named their sub-personalities (also called "alters"). Most gave names to various aspects inside themselves, and many reported the ages and genders of different parts. A group member said that her electric bill was cut off because she had a sub-personality who went to the mailbox and hid the mail from the conscious awareness of her more responsible parts. A man reported that he had a hard time going to the dentist, because sometimes the adult self would receive the anesthesia and the child self wouldn't. A woman found her days disrupted by driving to places she hadn't intended to go. She would start from home to go to the grocery store and end up coming back to awareness parked by the river at a nearby campground. A man with a part-time job was often reprimanded by his boss because while stocking shelves he'd sometimes become completely frozen for three to five minutes. His coworkers tried to get his attention, but they couldn't help him back to awareness. His condition disrupted his ability to date, drive, and stay connected to his extended family. He kept busy managing the split parts of himself that he called "the committee." As these survivors worked in therapy to integrate various aspects inside themselves, they had a tough process to go through. Some were able to blend and reintegrate their dissociative parts; others came to peace with their multiplicity and found strategies to function more effectively.[4]

Many trauma survivors dissociate while not having a full-blown dissociative personality disorder. As I have noted, memory is imprecise. Explicit memory is factual and contains linear thought and the capacity for us to tell stories about our past. It works well when the body is calm and at rest. It does not work well when the body is flooded with hormones or racing with impulses to fight, flee, or freeze. As Babette Rothschild notes in her book *The Body Remembers*, "In some cases, upsetting emotions, disturbing body sensations, and confusing behavioral impulses can all exist in implicit memory without access to information about the context in which they arose or what they are about."[5] These disturbances are often the first symptoms that trauma survivors notice.

Distress When Exposed to Traumatic Cues

Maury went to see a therapist because he didn't understand why he was anxious in bed every night. He would sometimes lie there for hours with this low-level shaking, "like the vibration function on my cell phone." His sleep loss led to irritability at work, and his last job performance evaluation was unusually low.

"I've always been in control," Maury said. He counted on emotional numbness to get him through life, often feeling very disconnected from his wife and two growing adolescents at home. "I can handle everything but this lack of sleep," he complained. Maury's lack of sleep seemed to him like a slippery slope into an out-of-control emotional world. And in a way, his interpretation was accurate.

As his therapist assessed his situation she asked Maury to describe his childhood. With his gaze set on the floor and his voice a near whisper, he said "I don't remember it."

"Most people think they should remember more than they actually do," his therapist said.

"Yeah, but don't they remember family vacations, meals together, going to the lake or fishing or something?" he pleaded.

"Yes, to varying degrees. How far back does your memory go?"

"I can remember high school, because I was on the football team and had a girlfriend, but not much before that."

"Tell me about your parents. What were they doing while you were younger?"

He sat up straighter for a moment. "My parents were fighting, my dad was drinking, my mom might have been having an affair, and who could blame her?"

His face became blank, and he stared at the ceiling in the office. She watched him dissociate.

"Maury," she asked very gently. "Where have you gone?"

He blinked a few times and looked over at her inquisitively. "Did I just say something?"

"Nope. You were just off somewhere in your thoughts—or trying not to think."

Maury had dissociative episodes "every now and then," but didn't know how to interpret its meaning or deal with it.

"Are they tied to my sleep problem?" He wanted to get back to a safer topic.

"They are likely connected, and with your permission, we'll start looking into the blank spots in your past once you can get a bit more control over your sleep and moments like the one you just had, when you seemed to disappear."

They set a plan together. Maury made a diary of his dissociative episodes, enlisting his wife and kids to help him with it. He learned to catch those episodes when they were just starting and to keep them from happening by using mindfulness, physical exertion, and biofeedback. But he still couldn't get to sleep—until the day he found the memory he'd been avoiding.

Maury's father had come home drunk one night. He pulled Maury's mother close with his elbow wrapped around her neck, screaming that he was going to get rid of her once and for all. Overhearing this, nine-year-old Maury emerged from his bedroom and watched his father lean back for a knife from the kitchen counter. His father yelled, "Go back to bed and just forget about this, or you can watch your mother die." Maury did what he was told. He lay on his bed shaking in fear that he would never see her again and feeling totally powerless to change the outcome he most dreaded.

Maury's mother thankfully survived and escaped her violent marriage. Maury survived by learning to forget. His forgetting entirely wiped out his childhood memories, and he grew up with a limited ability to identify or recall feelings. He didn't dare feel fear or anger, because they would link him back to a carefully buried memory. Other feelings shut down in the process—even the good ones he wanted to feel,

> Traumatic cues can include sights, sounds, tastes, smells, and times of day that replicate initial trauma states.

like love and joy. He carefully developed the coping strategy he most needed—to be in charge and in control. He avoided being out of control, because he equated it with becoming "just like my father." His mental condition wasn't as much an illness as an unconsciously improvised way to avoid trauma. It was effective for twenty-five years. And then, when he was mature enough, surrounded by safety and love, and secure in his work life, some symptoms showed up late at night and caught his attention. He was ready to begin the work of trauma recovery.

Many trauma survivors experience what are called trauma "cues." Maury's body held on to the night-time memory of shaking in bed. Another survivor, Mona, spent nearly five minutes every evening checking and double-checking her apartment door locks after an intruder broke in and ransacked her home. Traumatic cues can include sights, sounds, tastes, smells, and times of day that replicate initial trauma states.

A Concluding Note

While trauma disrupts people's memories with repression, dissociation, and intrusive recall, the brain also has the ability to re-create itself through a process known as neuroplasticity. All the victim/survivors I have described here had their memory systems disrupted. They each found ways to get past initial traumatic moments that could have destroyed their lives but didn't. Their symptoms had once helped them to adapt to their acutely stressful circumstances, and in recovery they learned ways to heal their scrambled, repressed, and intrusive memories. Their resiliency is inspiring.

I hope you came away from their stories, as I do, with great respect for the courage it takes to reconnect to disruptive memories, reframe experiences, and move forward.

For Reflection and Discussion

1 Think of a time when you experienced a loss or felt deep sadness. What physical symptoms were you aware of at the time?

2 Describe a dream that caused you to reexperience something traumatic.

3 How have your dreams helped you to cope with and resolve a problem?

4 Sometimes seemingly "odd" behaviors are actually coping strategies. What are your primary coping strategies when your stress is high?

3
Disrupted Moods and Behaviors

LET ME start with a note to trauma survivors. During and soon after a traumatic incident, as your brain began to calm down and take in all that just happened to you, you likely found that your feelings were harder to access or manage. The brain has a shut-off mechanism that acts like the GFCI switch (Ground Fault Circuit Interrupter) installed in a wall outlet to stop a dangerous overload of electricity. During intense fear, your brain instinctively knows how to disrupt normal response circuits and it shuts off your feelings to protect you. As one survivor told me, "I went someplace where no one could find me in the back of my brain, cut off and safe."

You may still find your feelings shutting down. This mechanism, which helped you survive in an untenable situation, often continues to turn your feelings off at times when they could be helpful. Recovery involves finding a way to get that on-off system to function properly. I hope that as you read the stories I've included here, you will find wisdom from other victims and experts in the field, and that you will find ways to become more comfortable managing your emotional world.

Remember Maury from the preceding chapter? Maury was so trauma-wounded by his father's rage that he became afraid of his own feelings. He had no role models to show him how to express sadness or vulnerability. He was scared that if he let his anger out, he would become violent like his father, so he ignored daily irritations and frustrations. The problem with Maury's strategy is that while he shut down the emotions he found unacceptable, all of his other emotions shut down too. He couldn't feel happy and loving emotions either. Maury gave up a lot when he made the unconscious decision to stay in emotional control. This strategy, which worked for him at the beginning, eventually needed to change. That's what happened to a woman I'll call Kari.

Kari was hired by a suburban church to fill in for their office secretary when she was out on maternity leave. As a mom with three school-aged children, Kari and her family needed the extra income. Bubbly and warm on the phone and friendly with people who dropped by the office, she seemed like a great fit for the job. What the people who decided to hire her did not realize is that Kari carefully disguised her trauma wounds.

Kari was raised by a single mom who pulled her out of school at age fourteen, just before her freshman year, and drove Kari and her ten-year-old brother from California to Florida. Kari's mom was searching for a job or a man to rescue them. When times got really tough, her mother sold Kari to men for sex and a "decent hotel room" for the night. Kari learned how to make it all look just fine on the outside in order to protect her younger brother, all the while fearing that her mother would utterly abandon them.

These traumatic wounds set the stage for lifelong mood and behavior disruptions. When she became frustrated, she would go from mildly annoyed to red-in-the-face rage in less than a minute. She often became loud and demanding at home. She knew this scared her children, and afterward she felt deeply remorseful, often retreating to her room and crying alone. These mood swings weren't brought on by a chemical imbalance; she did not have a bipolar disorder. Instead, her traumatic past had left her ill prepared to manage her moods. In psychology we use the term *dysregulation* to describe a person's inability to keep emotions in check.

Kari's volatility had caused her to lose several jobs, even though she had earned her GED and an associate's degree with skills in computer science and office management. The pastor who supervised Kari was puzzled about why someone so talented hadn't been able to keep her

> In psychology we use the term *dysregulation* to describe a person's inability to keep emotions in check.

previous jobs. She was personable on the outside, so what was the problem? It didn't take long for him to find out.

When Kari made minor mistakes in the weekly bulletin, she became overwhelmed with emotions. One morning, the pastor overheard her muttering to herself at her desk, saying, "I'm so stupid, I knew this job was too much for me, I can't even do small things without messing up." When the pastor asked her to do something differently one day, she fell into tears and apologized profusely—so much so that he was afraid to say anything at all to her for the rest of the day. She was still apologizing to him the next day for a mistake she'd caught and corrected the day before.

Situations that would normally roll off a person's back would entirely undo her. When a school nurse called to tell her that one of her children was throwing up and she needed to come get him, she flew into a rage on the phone. "I can't just walk away from my job. Can't you keep him in the office till after school? No, I don't have anyone else who can watch him!" Overhearing her conversation, the pastor encouraged her to take the rest of the day off. Without a word she closed out the computer, took her purse, and headed out the door. "Thank you," she yelled back as she went down the hall to her car.

> Labile emotions shift rapidly from one to another.

Kari's labile emotions were consistent with her traumatic wounding. Having spent her adolescence repressing her feelings, she couldn't figure out what to do with them in adulthood. Her emotions came out awkwardly. Her emotional age was more like thirteen—the age when her abuse began—so she acted and spoke more like she would have at her first school dance. In social environments she'd feel so shy and embarrassed that she couldn't express her feelings. She relied on being quiet and being nice. While these strategies worked for her in some ways, in others they didn't. She avoided confrontations with people, and the friends she chose repeatedly took advantage of her. Because she lacked skills in assertion and boundary setting, her children ruled the household. She had remained a child emotionally, and adult relationships were too risky to even try. While avoiding negative feelings, she blocked out positive feelings too. When her feelings came rushing to the surface quickly, she felt helpless and she couldn't contain them. She hadn't yet learned to use her feelings as helpful tools for a healthier and happier life.

Understanding Our Early-Warning Systems

For trauma survivors like Kari, signals that warn of impending danger become scrambled. Imagine that you are a pilot trying to become familiar with a new aircraft. Think about sitting in the cockpit with dozens of dials, lights, buttons, and levers in front of you. One of the first things you have to learn is what each of those dials and lights means and what system each button and lever activates. You have to learn how to distinguish one warning from another and how to respond to any alerts. Mistaking the red light that means the landing gear isn't working for the red light that means the lavatory door is ajar could be disastrous.

Now think of the buttons and levers on this cockpit instrument panel as your emotional system. You have many emotions to choose from, and they're all available to you. But you still have to know what each one means, how to activate or deactivate it—as well as what happens when you do. Trauma survivors frequently respond to all signals from the instrument panel as if they indicate extreme danger. They may mistake a small thing for a big or dangerous thing. This is how it was for Kari. Every negative signal from her emotional system's "instrument panel" activated warning lights in her brain. In the workplace Kari couldn't tell different warning systems apart. She became very confused and overwhelmed.

This is trauma's emotional toll. Kari's brain had been wired for threats in early adolescence when she experienced deep trauma. She didn't dare allow herself to feel anything when her body was being assaulted. How could she have felt secure on any given day when she didn't know when the next rape would occur? Her ability to effectively manage her fearful and anxious feelings was horribly damaged. When she felt vulnerable, this feeling led her directly to an all-encompassing feeling of shame. Her shame combined with

> For trauma survivors, signals that warn of impending danger become scrambled.

> You have many emotions to choose from, and they're all available to you. But you still have to know what each one means, how to activate or deactivate it—as well as what happens when you do.

> Many trauma survivors have to learn mood management skills. If they were traumatized as children and had poor parental role modeling, they are especially ill-equipped to sort out moods. Most victims learn to recognize emotions and use them appropriately through safe and protective relationships. Finding helpful role models, victims can learn emotional communication and emotional intelligence. A role model may be a relative, partner, church friend, pastor, or counselor.

her other out-of-control emotions left her to describe herself as "an emotional wreck."

Kari's survival strategies were no longer helping her; in fact, they were getting in her way. Her work at the church provided her with a bridge to wholeness. With her caring pastor's supervision and his patient workplace coaching, she grew more confident. She learned to slow down, speak kindly to herself, and get the pastor's help in order to determine the threat level at hand. Her job became her own version of pilot school, where she learned to identify separate emotions. She learned to turn switches on when needed and off when they were overfiring. Her maturation process, which had been cut short by years of trauma-induced shame, got back on track during a few months when she received clarity and grace.

Lessons from Freud

Sigmund Freud's seminal work as a physician launched the profession of psychotherapy and nearly all subsequent counseling methods. He introduced the world to the idea that what we think is happening right in front of us may be an overlay to protect us from less conscious and less pleasant realities. Freud noticed that following acute traumatic pain, his patients employed a consistent group of emotional strategies, including (among others) repression, projection, substitution, and denial.

I previously described the way Maury employed repression. When he buried his feelings, he could be temporarily free from their distraction and pain. Another way to avoid feelings is to project them onto someone else.

A common projection scenario goes like this. A woman gets frustrated on a long drive with her husband, because she wants to stop for a bite to eat and he wants to keep driving. She grows angrier when he gets quiet, and doesn't say anything for the next one hundred miles. She then says, "Are you angry with me?" and he says, "Nope," and stays silent because he's really not angry. In this case, she's the one who is angry and doesn't want to own her own angry feelings or be assertive about her needs. She projects her disowned anger onto him. The projection keeps her from expressing her own negative feelings.

Displacement operates in a similar way, by moving feelings onto something or someone else. A colleague at the university displaced her feelings of inadequacy onto the dean of her department. She was constantly irritated at his requirements for her courses—at having to learn new technologies and constantly update her lecture materials. Every requirement he made felt to her like an insult, which covered over her fear about being an imposter.

Another feeling avoidance strategy is substitution. Anger is a heroic emotion. It's the martial artist at work, and sometimes it functions as judge and jury. Anger substitutes for underlying feelings of vulnerability. When we are wounded, it's safer to get mad than to face pain and fragility.

Another substitution behavior is ingratiation. Abusers may apologize in sickeningly false ways in hopes of appeasing their victims. Children who have behaved badly may offer their parent a hug or seek reconnection through sing-song words and pretend contrition. Just think about a five-year-old repeatedly saying, "I'm sorry," albeit insincerely. It's safer to apologize than to face the angry parent.

Denial is the most well-known strategy trauma survivors use for emotional protection. Denial protects us from information that is too frightening to take in. Denial lets us block out overwhelming feelings for a while and then gradually, as we are ready, lets the truth sink in. People who have survived floods, train wrecks, or other near-death experiences will sometimes function quite well for a

> Denial lets us block out overwhelming feelings for a while and then gradually, as we are ready, lets the truth sink in.

while, using denial to push feelings out of conscious awareness. And then, when safety is reestablished, they can begin to feel their feelings.

Freud also developed the theory that in extreme cases of abuse trauma, a small number of victims will identify with their oppressors. This complex psychological condition, called the Stockholm Syndrome, was first named by criminologist Nils Bejerot after a bank robbery in Sweden in 1973. During the bank robbery with hostages, some of the hostages said they felt "safe" with their two captors and tried to negotiate for them with police. This syndrome has also been called trauma bonding. In situations of extreme duress, victims are so vulnerable that it's sometimes safest for them to align with their perpetrators in a series of complex mental and emotional maneuvers that keep fear at bay. While protective, this process can lead to months and years when a kidnapper keeps victims at his or her beck and call, despite emotional and physical abuse. This identification may be a victim's only means of survival.

While psychiatry and psychotherapy, beginning with Freud himself, have long pathologized our various complex emotional processes, they can be seen in a more graceful light. All of the victims I have worked with have found innovative ways to keep their emotions contained until safety and strength are regained. Victims tend to know when and how to begin letting their emotions into conscious awareness.

> Victims tend to know when and how to begin letting their emotions into conscious awareness.

When Mike went to see a therapist about his addicted and unfulfilled life, it took weeks for him to build enough trust to tell her what prompted his initial phone call. His denial had fallen away one morning while reading a local newspaper story about a registered sex offender who had moved into a house on his block. "I'm so appalled by this," he said. "How do I know if my grandchildren are going to be safe on my street? What will I tell them?" Finding the man listed on the state registry, Mike also learned that the offender had a felony for child rape. "I think there's a place in hell for a guy like that," he said. He

DISRUPTED MOODS AND BEHAVIORS

left the session stewing about what to do next. Mike was on the verge of a life-changing emotional breakthrough.

The next week he blurted out, "Why am I so appalled by that stranger down the street and still think about the man who molested me as an old friend?" Mike's therapist laid aside his notes, leaned forward a little bit, said simply, "I'm so sorry," and at that moment Mike's hard work began. Mike's defenses were crumbling.

Uncovering feelings takes great courage for trauma-wounded victim/survivors. In the process they may yet try to escape painful emotions. Survivors sometimes exchange one mood for another. Anger will step in to compensate for sadness. A mood like indifference will mask deep caring. Blame will substitute for shame. That's what Mike was doing when he felt intense fear and rage about the sex offender moving in on his block.

> Uncovering feelings takes great courage for trauma-wounded victim/survivors.

Trauma survivors need to understand the purpose for their protective strategies before changing them. Mike's emotional shutdowns had left him lonely and isolated from his family and friends, but they had also protected him from a complete emotional breakdown. While Kari's emotional reactivity was off-putting to others, it was also her assertive claim for justice, freedom from harm, and the right to have her needs honored and met.

Survivors' Rights

- I have a right to calmly and respectfully express my feelings.
- I may freely change my mind and my feelings.
- I have a right to feel differently from other people, including my friends and family.
- I claim my right to every feeling I experience, including strong ones and unpopular ones.
- I can live within my culture's norms about feelings or diverge from them.
- I have a right to keep my feelings to myself forever, or until I am ready to share them.
- I claim my feelings as valid and my worth as sacred.

The Avoidance Trap

When trauma survivors find the emotional load from their trauma too vexing, they can fall into an avoidance trap. These survivors substitute mood-changing activities for feeling genuine moods. Activities like drinking and drug use, and compulsive addictions to food, sex, gambling, hoarding, or social media all change dysphoric moods into highs and (albeit temporary) happiness. Anything that keeps the mind occupied for hours and that "numbs us out" is a way to keep unwanted feelings from coming up. The problem with avoidance is that it actually increases the power of that which is being avoided. "I was scared to get quiet and listen to myself," a survivor told me, "so I kept my mind as busy as possible and numbed myself with daily substance use."

> Dysphoria: The blue moods people feel when they are depressed.

Avoidance behaviors take us away from our desired goals and preferred values in order for us to reduce anxious or depressed feelings. A woman I'll call Nancy had a terrible car accident on a main thoroughfare in a suburban area. Nancy didn't want to drive near the scene where she had the car accident, so she'd go two miles out of her way to get to work, which cost her time and money. Every workday morning, she'd think, "Today I'll just go the direct route." Then her anxiety began to build, her heart started beating more quickly, and her palms began to sweat. She got a frantic feeling that she did not like, so she'd tell herself, "I might as well go the two miles out of the way. . . . I could do that forever if I wanted to." Instantly she felt calmer, and her body felt relief too.

Nancy was unintentionally reinforcing her avoidance. It feels good to be calm, and it feels bad to be anxious. Her feelings got to rule her day by asserting that she had more reason to avoid the direct route than to drive it. Next day, she went through the same thoughts and the same behavioral pattern, and the longer she did it, the more ominous the direct route felt.

Avoidance tries to protect trauma victims by allowing them to more gradually challenge the physical effects that arise when they are mentally reliving their traumatic moments. Psychologist Robert Grant writes gracefully about avoidance in his book on trauma recovery, *The Way of the Wound*.

> For many [trauma survivors] avoidance is not only the better part of valor, but a necessary part of healing. Victims know when understanding, support, safety, care and competence are unavailable. Most victims know when they, as well as others, are strong enough to deal with certain issues. . . . The psyche is wise and knows when it is appropriate to let down and face what was once considered to be overwhelming.[1]

Used consistently over time, avoidance strategies become more and more disabling. In Nancy's case, for example, her fear of driving past the scene of her accident grew larger rather than smaller. She began to fear any driving situation and to avoid other necessary trips like shopping for groceries and going to appointments. Until she learned to turn and face that road with response-prevention techniques, she became worse and worse. Nancy's assigned response-prevention techniques included deep breathing, using music for distraction, and verbal self-coaching with positive statements.

When addictions are used as avoidance strategies they can also escalate. More and more substance may be required to get the same level of emotional numbing. When the focus in life is getting high rather than getting healed, victims are heading in the wrong direction and need intervention. Recovery involves clearing away anything that keeps feelings from being discovered, felt, and expressed.

Shame and Trauma

I define shame as a deep sense of unworthiness in the sight of God or significant others. Among the emotions most trauma survivors carefully avoid, this is often the strongest and most influential. Shame is the underlying emotion when trauma takes place, and shame is the strongest and often last emotion to work through and

> Recovery involves clearing away anything that keeps feelings from being discovered, felt, and expressed.

> Shame is a deep sense of unworthiness in the sight of God or significant others.

heal. Shame has the power to immobilize victims by lowering their self-esteem, derailing their goals, and destroying their ability to imagine themselves being loved and accepted by relational partners.

Nancy shamed herself for being too "ridiculously weak" to drive directly to work, and because she often got there late, she shamed herself for that too. Kari shamed herself with verbal self-talk at work. "I'm no good, I'll never get this right, I'm a f--k up." Maury shamed himself for feeling unacceptable anger: "Just like my father, I could blow at any moment." Mike's sexual abuse shame led him to alcohol and daily marijuana use. The more he used, the more shame he experienced, and then the more he used. Thinking "I'm already lower than scum, so why not?" increases risk-taking behaviors that in turn increase shame. This is shame's downward spiral.

When a perpetrator inflicts trauma, shame becomes especially insidious. The shame that belongs on the perpetrator ends up on the victim in multiple situations. If the perpetrator is never confronted, or when confronted denies the abuse, the powerless victim is left with shame instead. For centuries, the shame that abusers ought to feel for their sexually predatory behaviors has been placed upon their victims. Women who are sexually abused are frequently told that they "invited" the abuse. "You must have egged him on," for example, or, "if you hadn't put yourself in that situation (had a drink, gone to his room, etc.) this wouldn't have happened to you." Blaming victims heaps shame on them while perpetrators wipe their hands and walk away. Where rape is minimized and victims are blamed, shame is too often thrown at them by close friends, family, congregants, coworkers, and social media.

> For centuries, the shame that abusers ought to feel for their sexually predatory behaviors has been placed upon their victims.

A colleague recently asked me whether the mainline church is a "rape culture," and I was astonished by this excellent question. Sociologists use the term "rape culture" to describe a cultural context in which rape is viewed as normal and expected due to attitudes about gender and sexuality. This concept includes victim blaming, denial or minimizing consequences, shaming victims, and trivializing abusive behavior. Phrases like "boys will be boys," "he

DISRUPTED MOODS AND BEHAVIORS   57

just couldn't help himself," and "she must have done something to egg him on," are typical sayings within a rape culture. There are elements of these old attitudes in nearly every church setting. Clergy sexual abuse survivors would likely say yes to my colleague's question. A pastor once told me, "We are a community of the shamed and the ashamed."[2]

In rape cultures, sexual assault victims clearly bear shame's brunt. Perpetrators may assert that their sex had been "consensual." If they acknowledge that they did something, they use minimizing words. They may also manipulate others through confession in order to elicit sympathy. In a remarkable interview about her rape at age seventeen by the youth pastor at her church, Jules Woodson and the *New York Times* prepared a film for the opinion page. She was asked to watch the video of her assailant making a confessional speech at his church and to offer her perspective. Red in the face and earnestly tearful, she describes her ongoing shame, made worse by the perpetrator's sympathy-drawing speech. Having spoken out, she was shamed by her faith community and strangers through social media. She titled her opinion for the *Times* "I Was Assaulted. He Was Applauded."[3]

Shame also has the power to create overachievers. Abuse victims may engage in compulsive overwork, seeking situations where overfunctioning helps them to overcome their shame. They go to great lengths to make up for their sense of being "damaged goods," setting the stage for burnout through constant striving to prove their own shame is wrong. These achievers neglect their own health and their families in their efforts to become more godlike and less tainted by the past. The person who becomes self-focused and image-focused is often a trauma victim trying to overcome his or her darkest secrets.

How then, does a trauma survivor heal shame? Recovery involves building a kind and loving relationship with oneself. Catching and correcting the negative self-talk is a good place to start. Healing includes self-talk that says, "I'm worth it," rather than,

> Healing includes self-talk that says, "I'm worth it," rather than, "I'm worthless." It includes making small behavior changes that move victim/survivors in the direction of their core values and beliefs.

"I'm worthless." It includes making small behavior changes that move victim/survivors in the direction of their core values and beliefs. This may mean adopting a fitness plan or practicing better sleep hygiene or eating habits. It may mean speaking up when undermined at work or catching and letting go of the tendency to prove worthiness through perfectionism.

When a trauma wound involves physical or sexual assault, shame cuts deeply into the soul. An abuse survivor carries scars that link directly to vulnerable emotions. This shame can be worked through by safe connection to a grace-providing family member, friend, or life partners. It can also be worked through by taking action steps to confront the assailant, as Jules Woodson did with Andy Savage. When perpetrators fail to take responsibility for their abuses and the traumatic wounds that continue, their victims heal by placing that shame back on the assailant where it belongs. Breaking secrets, speaking truths, and claiming the right to wholeness set the stage for healing.

The Joy of Healing

All emotions are purposeful. When trauma survivors become familiar with them, they can begin to listen to the messages within the emotions. "Why am I angry today?" "What does this sad feeling mean?" "I must be feeling vulnerable again." The questions may link back to old feelings that occurred or were repressed during traumatic experiences. In that case they point to scars that need healing. When the feeling is linked to current, new experiences, survivors can use them to identify their needs. Every strong feeling tries to be heroic in some way.

My colleague and fellow consultant William Kondrath has written a good book about feelings in faith communities. He writes, "Simply put, we have emotions because we need them. They give us messages about what is happening within and around us—messages that help us navigate life and make important decisions. God created

> Every strong feeling tries to be heroic in some way.

us as affectively competent beings."[4] Trauma-wounded people who have had this God-given gift damaged can still be healed.

Kari's ability to name her vulnerability helped during her work in the church front office. In shame-recovery with her therapist, she placed the shame and blame back onto her now-deceased mother for her neglect. She found a trusting support group and built new friendships. When her three months as substitute office secretary ended, she successfully found a permanent job. Maury learned to separate his own anger from the fear that he'd become his father and inflict similar damage on others. He surprised himself one day when he raised his voice at work and asked his boss for a long-overdue raise. Mike began a journey to fully release himself from the shame he felt for participation in sexual acts with his perpetrator, and he started a year's long process to claim legal and ethical justice from the church that covered up his abuse and failed to protect him. Nancy learned to drive to work and arrive on time with minimal stress. Befriending their own emotions led each of them to greater self-confidence and led them to positive emotions like hope and joy.

For Reflection and Discussion

1 Describe or write down some strategies you use to protect yourself when you feel vulnerable.

2 Which of your emotions do you most frequently rely on? Which do you avoid?

3 Consider a time when denial helped you or others in your family cope with a frightening situation.

4 The author asserts that anger is a strong feeling that tries to be heroic. When have you found this to be true?

4
Trauma's Damaged Relationships

TAKE A minute to think about someone you feel close to and safe with. Pick a person you feel pretty certain will never leave you, and who, if you journey off somewhere, will be at the door welcoming you when you return home. As you think about this person, notice what is happening in your body. Did you take a big breath? Did your shoulders relax? Did you feel other physical sensations? Some people doing this exercise feel warmth spreading through them. Others feel the stress of the day recede a little. Notice how your body feels when thinking about this person. And then take a moment to consider the emotions you experience when you think about this person. You may feel calm, vibrant, or content.

As I write this, I am thinking about my husband, who is a rock-solid person in my life. When I am with him a very subtle thing happens. The energy in my body flows more freely. And when we hug, heart to heart, until we both melt into it, our nervous systems relax. We are less on guard to the busy day, less alert for threats from a ringing phone, a broken garage door, or the "to do" lists in our heads. We can suspend our thoughts and just experience the warm hug physically and emotionally.

This is what the emotional bond called attachment feels like. In the words of therapist Susan Johnson, "If another stands beside you when you face overwhelming terror and helplessness—whether you name this terror . . . a 'dragon' or call it by some other name, such as traumatic stress—then everything is different." She notes that it's far easier to "defy the dragon" when you have someone beside you and you know that you are not alone.[1] An attached relationship provides solace and support. When you are securely attached to someone, you feel sure that you will not be abandoned. And you feel that even terrible life events can be endured.

Trauma Destroys Safety and Security

If you are a trauma survivor, you know the opposite feeling all too well. Immediately following your traumatic incident you felt isolated and alone, and you found it hard to feel safe with others. You likely found it hard to develop trust enough to be in any relationships, whether you were wounded by people you trusted or by strangers who dehumanized you. You may still find it hard to trust others. In this chapter I will be helping you to understand the disconnections you feel both physically and emotionally after trauma.

While you stand apart from people around you as you heal, it may seem that *everyone else* has safety and security in their relationships. If you have tried to heal your trauma wounds alone, without help or emotional support, you may feel even worse. I hope this chapter will show you a way to break out of silence when you are ready, and to consider the power that secure relational connection can offer.

Healing Connections

When trauma is borne alone, the isolation is also traumatizing. Since many traumatic wounds take place with only two people in the room, the violent perpetrator and the victim, the victim is essentially alone. Much trauma involves the loss of a loved one—the very one who had been the secure and dependable partner. This heart-wrenching loss cannot be felt by anyone else, not even well-intentioned others. When loneliness pervades the trauma, healing requires the victim/survivor to rebuild faith in dependable relationships.

> When trauma is borne alone, the isolation is also traumatizing.

It may be overly simplistic to say that all species need dependable relationships, but I'm going to risk saying it anyway. I worked a few years at a zoo, where it became clear to me that sticking together for survival is not unique to human beings. Elephants grieve with heartbreaking beauty. Wolves mope around in what looks like depression when one of them dies. Watching a mother, whether a lioness or a meerkat, protect her young, we witness the attachment phenomenon.[2] In the wild, animals protect the vulnerable in their groups by surrounding them with strong allies. When an animal is alone, its risk of death goes up. We are no different. Our brain circuitry is hardwired for attachment.

After my parents both died within nine months of each other, I had a series of physical concerns that sent me rushing to a medical doctor for evaluation. Luckily, she found nothing to worry about, but I did learn that I was at increased risk for life-threatening health conditions in the first two years following my parents' deaths. If my loss had been a spouse or a long-term partner, my risk of developing major health issues would have gone up within the first thirty days after that loss.[3]

Many theorists believe, and research has shown time and time again, that attachment strongly affects our ability to cope with excessive stress. Johnson explains, "The attachment system is evolution's way of maximizing survival in a dangerous world, a world in which a person cannot survive alone."[4] Our attachment to a trusted person can also help us to restore the lost sense of identity that occurs during trauma.

Early Studies in Attachment

Attachment theory was first formulated by British psychologist John Bowlby in the 1960s. He and his colleague and fellow researcher Mary Ainsworth studied infants with their mothers and developed schemas about different attachment styles within these relationships. They assigned mothers with twelve- to eighteen-month-old babies to leave the room and observed the children through a one-way mirror. What did the babies do when they were left with a stranger? Did they cry? Did they stare blankly off into space? Did they seek a toy?

And then they watched carefully to see what the babies did when their mothers returned. Did the baby rush to greet her with open arms, cry, giggle, or turn away and ignore her as if to say, "You walked out on me and I can't trust you anymore!"? Then they analyzed and categorized the babies' responses. They described the babies as primarily secure (calm and happy to reconnect with mother), anxious-avoidant insecure (avoiding or ignoring mother upon her return), and anxious-resistant insecure (demonstrating anxiety about exploring the environment). In rare instances, a baby exhibited a combination they called disorganized-disoriented. Many studies have replicated Ainsworth and Bowlby's results.

Researchers in the field of psychiatry continued to study attachment theory and found that adult relationships tend to follow similar patterns. The patterns are more commonly known today as secure, anxious, and avoidant. According to psychiatrists Amir Levine and Rachel Heller, in their book *Attached*, "Just over 50 percent [of adults in relationships] are secure, around 20 percent are anxious, 25 percent are avoidant and the remaining 3 to 5 percent fall into the fourth, less common category (combination anxious and avoidant)."[5] Their studies and writings help adults find ways to identify secure partners for dating and long-term relationships. Using attachment theory, they help people who have repeatedly been unsuccessful in their search for partnership identify their anxieties and avoidance patterns, so that they can instead find and create secure attachment.

Edward Tronick, a developmental psychologist, studied the importance of mirroring in attachment. When using the term "mirroring," psychologists are referring to behavior controlled by neurons in the brain that can mirror feelings. These mirror neurons help us to have empathy. They light up inside our brains in such a way that we actually pick up on another's feelings as they tell us

> When using the term *mirroring*, psychologists are referring to emotional behavior controlled by neurons in the brain. When observing feelings in someone else, the observer's brain elicits similar feelings.

about them or show them through facial expressions, flushes, or tears. Mirror neurons help us to feel similar feelings.

Tronick developed an experiment in which a mother first mirrored her child and then turned away. His videos of babies and parents interacting in these experiments are available several places online. The videos' popularity stems in part from the fact that as adults we still have an inner child, and that child needs mirroring from loved ones. I recommend Tronick's video clips for adult couples who want to understand the power of a closely connected relationship.[6]

In the Tronick "Still Face Baby Experiment," we see a mother sitting close to and directly across from a baby in an infant car seat. The baby is about six months old. The mother is looking warm and engaged. She's following the child's every expression and mirroring those expressions with her own face. The child points, the mother points. The child giggles, and the mother giggles. The mother is then asked by the researcher to turn her face away and look back at the child without expression. She doesn't mirror the baby for a whole minute, and in just a few seconds the baby begins to disintegrate emotionally. She tries to get her mother to engage in their usual game, pointing, and looking at her. When the mother remains flat faced, the baby screeches, loses body posture, and begins to sob uncontrollably. At that point, the mother is instructed to return to her baby with eye gaze, mirroring, and soothing behaviors, and the baby returns to his former happy state.

Even as adults, we need the people around us to notice and respond to our emotional expressions. This basic interaction calms the central nervous system and enhances a felt sense that everything is okay in the world around us. Without it, we can continually get stuck in panic mode.

How Adult Attachment Works

Attachment underlies our ability to develop properly, form friendships to lighten the load, and form significant loving relationships. Working with couples, Susan Johnson has extensively

> We need the people around us to notice and respond to our emotional expressions.

studied the central tenets of attachment theory, which I've condensed and adapted for our purposes. While trauma wounds damage primary relationships, safely secure primary relationships give space for those wounds to heal.

We Are Designed for Attachment

We all need to be close to those we love, and we all fail to thrive when this love is withheld or disappears. While psychology has long pathologized people for their dependency (for example, labeling someone as having a dependency disorder and referring them to a codependency recovery programs), our dependency is built into our biology, just as it is in the animal kingdom. Staying close is protective.

We Can Be Both Securely Attached and Autonomous

When partners are close and securely attached, there is room in their relationship for autonomy. A troubling scripture for many couples is Jesus's comment in Mark 10:8 that "the two shall become one flesh. So they are no longer two, but one flesh." This text evokes a fear that we will be swallowed up into the other. It can make a marriage seem like obliteration. We can't exactly tell the context in which Jesus proposes this, but if he's describing that we become each other's advocates, rocks, places of solace and safety, then I'm all for it. We do not lose our autonomy when we are secure. In fact, we are able to wander off and return without anxiety. We can be left behind or be alone without fear that we have been abandoned. Couples in secure attachments come together joyfully, and when they are apart they feel secure and self-confident. In Johnson's words, "The more connected we are, the more separate and different we can be."[7]

We Find Safety in Secure Attachment

When life changes, leaving us feeling vulnerable, we seek refuge in other people. Multiple studies have shown that when women are feeling insecure or in danger, they go searching for connection.

They "tend and befriend." Women are relationally acculturated and affirmed for their close and nurturing relationships. But women are not alone in their need to tend and befriend. Research shows that all genders need this, and in times of stress all genders seek connection. Positive attachments are mentally and emotionally protective, and we instinctively know this.

Secure Attachment Involves Being There for Each Other

In a Hold Me Tight workshop for couples with Rebecca Jorgenson, my husband and I learned to offer each other three basic responses that are summed up in the word *are* in the question, "*Are* you there for me?" "A" stands for accessible, "R" for responsive, and "E" for engaged. All of these responses add up to security. Even when expressing negative emotions like anger, a couple who engage in respectful dialogue can remain attached.

Not too long ago I was in the kitchen chopping vegetables and accidentally took a slice off my finger. "Ouch," I wailed. My cry seemed loud to me, but my husband had his headphones on and was listening to music in the other room. I rushed to the sink to rinse my finger off and assess the damage. "Hey," I said, feeling like the abandoned baby in Tronick's experiment. "Come out here. I've hurt myself." And then angrily, "Didn't you hear me?" I still had no partner at my side, but by then I knew that I wasn't going to need stitches and the throbbing had eased a little.

I wrapped my finger in a paper towel and went to the other room—still seeking my partner's comfort. As he looked up, he saw my angry red face and thought to himself, "I've done something wrong. . . . Uh oh." We might have stayed distant and cold, but he set aside his fears that he was in trouble with me, stood up, opened his arms, and drew me toward him. He noticed the paper towel and the blood and became very accessible, responsive, and engaged. I could then say, "I needed you." And he could say, "I'm sorry I wasn't right there when you called." Understanding that he wanted to help me allowed me to lower my anger and reconnect.

This is how attachment works with small stuff, and it works that way with the big stuff too. We learned the way this works at the workshop, and we practice it a lot. We regard each other's well-being and protect each other's well-being through connection. Our trainer told us that we can turn either toward our partner or away from our partner. When we don't show up emotionally for each other, we spiral into emotional reactivity. My husband and I are far from perfect in our attempts at connection, but even our clunky tries are better than not showing up emotionally at all.[8]

Renowned couple's therapist John Gottman has identified several ways that relationships get into serious trouble, but the most egregious he calls "stonewalling"[9]—the opposite of being accessible, responsive, and engaged. When partners stonewall, they are feeling so hopeless about making a secure attachment that they avoid repeated disappointments by detaching.

We Need Attachment Even More When Fear and Uncertainty Arise

When we feel uncertain, are injured, or face stresses in our daily lives, we have more need to attach. When newborn infants in their first anxious moments are laid on their mothers' breasts, they know instinctively to turn toward a nipple. On their fathers' chests they instinctively cuddle up to experience the comfort of two hearts beating together. This turning toward nurturance remains with us throughout our lives—far beyond the breastfeeding stage. Trauma survivors instinctively search for connection.

We Are Likely to Be Distressed When We Are Separated

Beneath many dynamics in couples' relationships lies a desperate demand for connection. What happens when we lack secure attachment? We engage in predictable behaviors such as "anxious clinging, pursuit, and even aggressive attempts to obtain a response from the loved one."[10] A wise mentor once told me, "All anger is a demand for love." It's like a screeching baby whose parent has turned away when needed. I asked a client one time after he went on a rant against his partner in therapy, "Do you want to be right, or do you want to be close?" and he said, "Both." Yet underneath his demanding adult self-righteousness lay a very insecurely attached child who wanted to be understood, valued, and held. We all do.

The Search for Safety and Security

Understanding these concepts in attachment theory, we can look again into the aftermath of trauma. When I was in the airplane that nearly crash-landed, I was a little nutty (or we could say instinctively aware) about needing attachment. The young man next to me sought me out too. He looked me in the eye from time to time, something strangers on airplanes don't commonly do. And when I asked him if I could hold his hand as the plane was racing toward a rocky and uncertain landing, (which I would never have done under ordinary circumstances) he seemed quite glad to oblige. We both thereby lowered the blaring alarm systems going off in our bodies and calmed our panicky thoughts.

After a loved one dies, we commonly turn to those who were also close to that loved one for solace. A grandmother, losing her son, moved to another community to be closer to his children. A grieving young bride, whose husband was killed in Iraq, moved in with his parents for a while to share memories and grief. After losses, we instinctively seek closeness with those who can provide emotional links. We need and seek connection.

When I was working late as the emergency room chaplain, I was called in one night to be with a family whose young daughter had been run over and killed. A psychologist came and offered a trauma debriefing group for the medical providers on staff, but I got no such debriefing. I stayed in the room with the mother, father, and child and kept the coroner at bay for hours while they grieved. I went home at four in the morning, feeling wrung out from the emotional weight within me, and phoned my sister. Luckily it was seven a.m. her time, and she listened to me for quite a while and went in to work late. She provided me with secure attachment. Bowlby's work on attachment showed that when we have someone who can be there for us when needed, we are "much less prone to either intense or chronic fear than an individual who has no such confidence."[11]

How Hugging Heals

Secure couples calm down each other's nervous systems. Daily physical contact, such as handholding and hugging, enhances the functioning of the parasympathetic nervous system. In secure relationships we become more capable of self-soothing. Trauma survivors with secure partners find that they become less and less reactive when they are triggered by past memories or intrusive thoughts. The partner's reassuring words, "It'll be okay," can lower the survivor's perception of threat. Earlier, I described the need for a trauma survivor to recognize the warning lights in the airplane cockpit in order to safely travel in the world. The partner becomes the cognitive and emotional copilot in safely secure relationships. The partner who knows how to tell the difference between the red warning lights can help the survivor assess the threat level and act

---

The following table from Susan M. Johnson's *Emotionally Focused Couple Therapy with Trauma Survivors* lays out traumatic symptoms and the healing provided by secure attachment.

Traumatic Experience	**Secure Attachment**
Floods us with physical fear/helplessness.	Soothes and comforts.
Colors the world as dangerous/unpredictable.	Offers a safe haven.
Creates overwhelming emotional chaos.	Promotes affect regulation/integration.
Threatens a cohesive sense of self.	Promotes personal integration.
Assaults self-efficacy and a sense of control.	Promotes confidence/trust in self and others.
Scrambles the ability to engage fully in the present, and so to adapt to new situations.	Promotes openness to experience, risk-taking, and new learning.[12]

accordingly. When the survivor goes into panic and yells, "What do we do, a warning light is on?" the secure partner can say, "Hey, it's okay, we'll figure it out together," or slow down the reactive process by handholding or hugging.

Hugging and cuddling release oxytocin in the brain. This is known as the love and bonding chemical. Hugs increase dopamine in the brain, flooding us with a sense of well-being and satisfaction. Hugs increase serotonin availability, which is what antidepressant drugs are designed to do. Our skin-to-skin contact conducts electricity and moisture, which balances the nervous system. Hugs decrease the cortisol-induced stress responses we feel every day when frustrations arise. To risk an old seventies cliché, our bodies hum with "good vibrations"!

In an exercise for couples, Stan Tatkin, who developed a program called a Psychobiological Approach to Couple Therapy (PACT) suggests that when partners leave each other and return home to each other they should hug, heart to heart, until their bodies relax. This allows them to regulate their adrenal systems. No matter what the partner at home is doing, that partner needs to stop, go to the one returning home and offer the hug. This habit alone has healed many couples and kept them grounded in the midst of daily stress.[13]

> While hugs from trusted intimate partners are healing, unwanted hugs from strangers, people in authority, pastors, and even friendly people at church can retrigger trauma and disrupt healing. Hugging can be abusive within intimate partnerships and between coworkers and acquaintances. Never presume that a person needs a hug or would be helped by a hug, because an unwanted hug will trigger the wrong set of physiological responses. Hugs provide positive benefits only in situations of full consent and mutuality. Unwanted touch induces rather than heals trauma.

When Secure Attachment Is Lost

When trauma wounding involves the death of a partner, grief is experienced as physical withdrawal. Grieving lovers describe their evenings and overnights as excruciatingly lonely. They can't reach over for a hug or embrace at the time they need this comfort the most. A body pillow, an old shirt the loved one wore, or other comfort object can help a grieving partner, but the biochemicals that their brains released when they were touched by their lover go crazy looking for their lost mates. Both heart and body keep trying to secure their bonded attachment to no avail. The loss of close attachment is devastating.

When Ralph lost his wife to a tragic automobile accident, he experienced the double whammy of grief and trauma. They had been so securely attached that he felt the disconnection mentally and physically. His self-perception had been tied to being Laura's husband for forty-two years. He didn't know how to structure his day, plan social activities, or sleep alone at night. "I'm just so lost," he told their adult children. "I rattle around in this old house, and she is everywhere and nowhere all at the same time." His children became alarmed after he seemed depressed for more than a few months and sent him to his medical doctor for a checkup. Blood work came back without abnormality; his blood pressure was a little high but could be controlled. "Ralph," his doctor said, "what you are missing is companionship. You may not be ready to date, but you have to get out and be around people sometimes. Take a trip, go stay with your kids for a while." Ralph went away unconvinced.

A few months later he joined a fitness challenge at his local YMCA to lose a little weight, and it drew him into connection with a trainer and a team of people with similar goals. This lifted his mood when he was at the gym, but he still felt acutely lonely at home. Ralph's usual way to handle stress was to turn to Laura for reassuring connection. Now, when he was overwhelmed and uncertain, he had no one to turn to. "I just miss her hugs," he told his daughter.

He used the word "just" in his comment about missing her hugs, as if this were no big deal. However, his loss of secure attachment was a big, big deal. The hug that connected him to Laura had helped him regulate his nervous system for decades. She always had his back and helped him when he became uncertain, and they shared decision-making. Now, he found it hard to calm himself down when he was anxious about his future and distraught in grief. She had been the source of his security.

Ralph grieved Laura, and he grieved the loss his body felt when he wasn't being held regularly. His bodily cravings for her seemed like drug withdrawal to him. Ralph's doctor knew this when he advised him to connect with people. And while Ralph was skeptical that day, he took his doctor's advice and set out to intentionally meet new people. After a fitness class at the gym, he asked a woman named Rita to join him for coffee. They are now heart hugging.

Singles can build satisfying relationships in which to be held too. Women, more easily than men due to their acculturation, often bond with friends who offer hugs and cuddling, particularly during grief. How else can people experience the benefits that touch provides? Stroking a pet can release stress and increase the pleasure chemistry in the brain. Massage therapy awakens those "good vibrations" too.

Childhood Trauma's Effects on Adult Physical Health

On the last day in a class I was teaching on abnormal psychology, I asked students what they had learned in the course. A student's hand shot up and I recognized her. "I had no idea how much adult mental health is connected to childhood trauma," she said. At that

> Insurance companies are becoming wise about the preventative and restorative care massage offers and some now pay for it. Check with a local chiropractic office to find a massage therapist who could see you under your medical plan. Massage schools are good places to find low-cost massages.

moment I was satisfied that my teaching had been life-changing for the class. Understanding the connection between adult wellness and adverse childhood experiences, these counselors in training will have greater compassion for those who are suffering. And, hopefully, students in the classroom will also have greater compassion for their own struggles.

We cannot underestimate the toll childhood trauma takes across the lifespan. In the eighth grade I was at summer camp on a hike. When we got to a rocky overlook I held onto a small tree and leaned forward. The tree was not secure and I fell forward over the ledge. My left leg hit a dirt pathway—keeping me from plunging farther over the cliff. But the impact broke both bones in my left leg, as the doctor said, "clean through."

I'd call this a trauma with a small "t," and I eventually fully recovered. My body was still growing and strong. With the help of a huge cast, my bones healed and I was back to normal functioning after about six months. But the bruise on my leg remained tender and discolored for two dozen more years.

By adulthood I was the only one who knew I'd been damaged. When it rained, I felt dull aches at the point where my leg broke. When I jumped on that leg a certain way, it sent pain shooting up into my thigh. To everyone around me I looked just fine, even in dancing classes and during performances. I was the only one who knew that lingering damage remained. This experience is what trauma survivors report to me. They look okay to the outside world, but they still carry unseen scars. Sometimes old pain comes surging through the body and the brain, calling out alert signals. Years after traumatic wounding, changes in the brain and the body often go unnoticed by others, while trauma victims privately know their wounds remain.

The psychiatric community previously overlooked some chronic long-term symptoms in people whose childhoods were marked by physical, emotional, or psychological abuse. In the 1980s, Dr. Vincent Felitti, now director of the California Institute of Preventive

> Years after traumatic wounding, changes in the brain and the body often go unnoticed by others, while trauma victims privately know their wounds remain.

Medicine, became curious about ways that his patients' life histories affected their wellness. Felitti was treating obese women at his clinic. He observed that while he could help them lower their weight, keeping the weight off was much more difficult. He went looking for clues after two of his patients reported having been abused as children. This prompted him to interview other patients, and he found that over half of his weight-loss patients had histories of child sexual abuse trauma. He joined Dr. Rob Anda for a study of 17,000 patients, and they were both surprised and saddened by the findings. In his study of mostly middle-aged, white upper- and middle-class patients from San Diego, California, he found that one in ten had experienced domestic violence, two in ten had been sexually abused, and three in ten had been physically abused.

The study questionnaire the doctors used is now called the ACE, Adverse Childhood Experiences, survey. The ten-question survey, available on the internet,[14] addresses abuse, neglect, and household dysfunction and is widely used in assessments by mental health providers and medical providers.

The results exceeded the researcher's initial hunches. "Just the sheer scale of the suffering—it was really disturbing to me," Anda recalled.[15] When he compared their abuse histories with their medical conditions, he was astonished. A long list of diseases, including addictions, cancer, diabetes, and stroke, occurred more often among people with high ACE scores.

A National Public Radio story about the research reports, "According to the findings, adults who had four or more 'yeses' to the ACE questions were, in general, twice as likely to have heart disease, compared to people whose ACE score was zero. Women with five or more 'yeses' were at least four times as likely to have depression as those with no ACE points."[16] Clearly mental health issues are high among people with trauma histories, but this study showed poorer physical health outcomes as well. Patients with higher scores have an increased risk for physical, mental, and social dysfunction later in life. This study provides more evidence leading to Susan Johnson's staunch advocacy for relational health as the healing balm for trauma.

While high scores raise concerns, they are not predictive. Mitigating factors in childhood abuse and trauma are believed to play a role too. People who had positive role models outside the family—a protective grandparent, teacher, church mentor, or neighbor—may not manifest as many physical symptoms in later life as those without mitigating factors. The ACE score sheet can alert the physician to the stress level the patient may be experiencing due to chronic PTSD, which is oftentimes underreported and untreated. Some patients with moderate or high scores have developed immunity protections over time. By living healthy lifestyles, not smoking, exercising frequently, eating and sleeping well, and seeking therapy, they have mitigated their physical and mental health risks. By creating secure and safe relationships, they have also lowered their risk of negative physical outcomes.

Congregations Nurturing Secure Attachment

A faith community can provide a supportive environment for relational connection. When visitors walk through the front door of a church, they may be seeking relational closeness. Will they find a small group or one-on-one significant friendships? Assuming that a new visitor is asking, "Are you there for me?" how might a congregation be sure that every person who attends gets connected to a dependable person within that community, who is accessible, responsive, and engaged? This connection cannot be left solely to the pastor. And clergy who try to be relationally connected to everyone are on the road to burnout and falsely narcissistic egoism.

In congregations, lay servant-leaders are sometimes the first to learn about childhood traumas and the first to build trust with trauma-wounded individuals. How can unprofessionally trained but caring people help those who have lived through adverse childhood experiences? The first thing a congregation needs to do to create safety for trauma survivors in groups is to establish safety and trust. Small-group leaders need to establish guidelines that limit information sharing outside of the group and teach members to offer support without gossiping about heartfelt disclosures. Clergy and small-group leaders are not trained or equipped to provide therapy, but they can offer prayer and referrals to programs that will help. Clergy do more harm than good by trying to be too intimately involved in the healing of trauma-wounded parishioners. They can help, however, by carefully assessing their parishioners' vulnerabilities and resiliency and then offering appropriate referrals.

It is essential that clergy and lay leaders keep clear boundaries about their time and emotional investment while caring for trauma-wounded congregants. Providing too much emotional intimacy could be confusing and frightening to a trauma survivor, leading to romantic transference or dependency. This attachment might be seen in behaviors like incessant phone contact, calling about "crises" that could actually be handled later, asking for more time than the pastor or leader has available to give. Then, when clergy or lay leaders set reasonable limits, the trauma-wounded person may respond by feeling dejected and abandoned. These complicated dynamics need to be managed by counselors with significant training. Trauma-informed individual and couples therapists are uniquely qualified to address past trauma. I advise every clergyperson to become well acquainted with therapists and resources in their communities to whom they can make referrals.

Within the congregation, programs where groups work together for a common goal are good starting places for people who need to connect. Working alongside others is a safe way to build relational trust. Whether pulling weeds together on the church lawn, cooking for an event, or helping at a food bank, a shared volunteer experience is often a great place for people to create safe attachment for the first time in their lives.

After the #metoo movement began, several clergywomen started groups to bring together harassment and abuse victims. One pastor formed a mending circle, where the art of darning old clothing became a place for metaphorically and literally mending

TRAUMA'S DAMAGED RELATIONSHIPS 77

life wounds. Another pastor recruited a retired therapist to form a survivor group to address the past with an eye toward a fully healed future.

How It All Comes Together

Gabriella checked a box on my office intake form indicating that she was a Christian, but she had also added a question mark after the box. After a few months into her therapy for childhood sexual trauma, I felt it was time to ask her more about her faith background. She had gone to church as a child and found it satisfying. And so I asked, "Do you pray?"

"I used to," she said. "As a child I used to kneel by my bed at night and pray that Daddy wouldn't come home drunk again and come into my room to mess with me at night. I prayed this often, but it didn't really work, so by the time I became an adult I gave up prayer altogether. It seemed like God had abandoned me too."

"I can understand that. You needed God to stop the monster in your room."

"Exactly. My wife, Julie, is more available to me than God seems to be at this point. She knows how to hold me and reassure me that I'm okay. She says that we'll be okay no matter what happens. Fifteen years with her has given me a safe place to be myself. I also know she wants what's best for me." After a long pause, Gabriella added, "I guess that's what I want from God!"

"Exactly," I said. "Would you ever feel like you could take up a conversation with God about this? Maybe, let God know how hard it was for you to be abandoned when you were so vulnerable?"

"I sure wouldn't be able to call God my 'Father,'" she said. "If there is a God, abuse is not part of the plan. Grace and love are."

"What if you called God by what you need most?"

She smiled. She said, "I'd start like this. Oh, Non-abandoning One, hear me out. . . . I've actually got a lot to say!"

Gabriella, a lovely and wise person, showed me the way that trauma survivors begin to create and re-create secure attachments, with God, with spouses and partners, with family members and friends.

For many trauma survivors, every place feels unsafe, and every relationship is suspect. This is a difficult paradox, because trauma-wounded survivors (like all of us) need to have people around them who will respond with care when called upon and who will offer grace to heal lingering shame. Healing begins when survivors fully accept that they are innately vulnerable and needy, and claim their right to safety and support. Healing includes asking their partners, friends, and God, for the safety and security they need. In Gabriella's situation it included the need to repair her relationship with God and then to demand that she be heard and cared for.

Whenever we feel fear and uncertainty arise, attachment seeking makes good sense. Touching, wrestling, clinging, and delighting in each other are very human behaviors that are hardwired into us from birth. Sometimes, when the weight of the world feels very overwhelming, we find hope by reaching out for a hand to hold or step closer to a secure loved one to be safely enfolded. Our bodies relax, and then our bodies send a message to the brain that says, "It will be alright."

For Reflection and Discussion

1 Recall a time when having someone's hand to hold made all the difference for you.

2 Watch the "Still Face Baby Experiment" on YouTube or on the Gottman Institute website (see endnote 9 for this chapter). Then discuss what you felt while watching the mother and baby interacting.

3 How would you define a "secure attachment"?

4 Hugs can hurt, and hugs can heal. What has been your experience with hugs?

> Whenever we feel fear and uncertainty arise, attachment seeking makes good sense.

Part Two
Types of Trauma

5

When Trust Is Betrayed: Child Sexual Abuse Trauma

Briana stood at the back of the hall as everyone gathered for a workshop on child sexual abuse. Participating counselors and schoolteachers grabbed their information packets and found their way to seats at long tables facing the podium. But Briana stayed near the back door, leaning uncomfortably against the door jam. I wondered why.

She was about five feet tall and had shoulder-length brunette hair. She wore cowgirl boots, a long skirt, and jacket we could call "business casual." She was bi-racial and looked to be in her late forties. During the presentation she paced back and forth, reminding me of caged animals I had watched at the zoo. Was she, perhaps, physiologically overcharged by the material being presented?

Nearing the lunch break, the lecturer said that children are safer from abuse in a home when both parents are around. I have no recall of the context for that sentence, because Briana went into overdrive. She rushed forward, grabbed a floor microphone, and said:

> I want you to know how little time it takes to rape a child. My parents were both home, and they had friends over. My father went to the bathroom and came out into my room, shoved me against the wall, pulled down my pants, put his hand over my mouth, and raped me. It took less than a minute. I could hear my mother's voice on the other side of that wall. It happens *so much faster* than you think. I just want you to remember that.

The room fell silent. She walked to the beverage table at the back of the room, got a glass of water, and for the first time that day, sat down in an end-row seat. The presenter thanked her and resumed her lecture. I caught Briana's name on her tag at the lunch break.

Briana was so vulnerable and yet so courageous, and as hard as her story was to hear, I haven't forgotten her. Her strong witness and her powerful trembling voice provided the participants in the room with more lasting education than all the other content put together. I left the training day having learned that I dare not assume anything. I have to open my heart and listen. Victims are our wisest teachers.

> Victims are our wisest teachers.

The Extent of the Problem

Most sources estimate that one in three women and one in five men have been sexually abused by the age of twenty-five. These numbers vary according to regions, and are largely culled from police reports, child protective services, and therapists. Statistics about gender differences in abuse may not be entirely accurate. More women than men go to therapy; therefore, more data are collected about them. Men face a double dose of shame about their abuse and their failure to be "man enough" to have stopped it. They are acculturated to deny more and report less. Many men and some women are coerced by siblings or peers into participation in group sexual activity, including abuse. Those who are forced to watch rape and are powerless to stop it end up very deeply distressed.

While the numbers may not fully tell the story about sexual abuse trauma victims, we can identify some groups of people who are at greater risk than others. Children (those under age eighteen) with gender ambiguity or who express same-sex attractions are at higher risk than their gender-conforming peers. When a girl is being abused in a family, boys in that same family are often targeted for physical or sexual abuse too. Stepchildren are at higher risk of all forms of abuse than biological children. Children with physical or mental disabilities are at higher risk for sexual abuse than other children.

> The Scope of the Problem
>
> According to the National Children's Alliance:
>
> - Nearly 700,000 children are abused in the US annually.
> - A thousand or more children die from abuse annually.
> - Over three million cases are reported to child protective services each year for investigation.
> - Seventy-seven percent of perpetrators are one or both of the child's parents.[1]

According to statistics from Darkness to Light, a nonprofit resource for survivors of child sexual abuse and their communities, race and ethnicity play a role in increased incidents of child sexual abuse. African American children have almost twice the risk of sexual abuse of white children across all economic strata, and children with Hispanic ethnicity have a slightly greater risk than non-Hispanic white children.[2] Many children have more than one of these risk factors to contend with.

Most abuse takes place in family homes or in the homes of perpetrators. Sexual abuse and incest have more to do with the availability of the child than the child's race, gender, or other characteristics. Perpetrators choose victims by sizing up their vulnerability. Finding a wounded, lonely, or isolated child, an abuser identifies that child as an "easy target." My experience as a therapist has taught me that anyone who is perceived to be "different" in a family is more likely to be the target of abuse.

If you, like Briana, experienced sexual abuse in your home as a child, and if you were abused in the home of a neighbor or at church, I hope that these statistics help you to realize that you are not alone. You did not deserve the violence you experienced, no matter the color of your skin, your gender identification, your abilities or disabilities. The way you expressed your feelings and ways you behaved aren't the reason for your abuse, nor was your place and role in the family. *The predatory behavior of your perpetrator had*

> Anyone who is perceived to be "different" in a family is more likely to be the target of abuse.

more to do with your availability than any other characteristic. And your home, neighborhood, or church, which should have been a safe place, wasn't safe for you, which is extremely traumatic. I hope that this chapter helps you to feel less isolated, less to blame, and more empowered as we turn our focus toward healing.

Developmental Delays

When children are physically or sexually traumatized, their emotional and relational development is delayed. A one-time sexual abuse incident can lead to a lifetime of fear and mistrust; repeated incidents will alter the child's life course. When personal integrity, safety, and life itself are threatened during childhood, brain development, including the capacity to organize thoughts and regulate feelings, is disrupted. When a child's abuser is a parental figure, or a parent participates through failure to protect, the victim's attachment becomes random, chaotic, and avoidant.

When Mack was five his parents got divorced, and the judge decided to divide the siblings in the family. His older sister went with their mom, who moved to another state. He moved into an apartment with his dad near the elementary school. After Mack started acting oddly at school his teacher called his mom and learned that his parents had divorced. His teacher watched his appearance and moods change over the next six months. Once talkative with peers, he pulled into a shell and often hung out alone on the playground near the fence. Then she noticed something alarming: he wore long-sleeved shirts every day in the springtime—even when temperatures reached into the high seventies. She asked him if everything was alright at home and he said "Yes," but he didn't make eye contact. During an assignment when students drew pictures of their families, Mack drew a mom and dad and himself standing in their yard.

"Is this your mom and dad? Have you drawn your family like it used to be?" she asked.

He pointed to the woman in the drawing. "No, that's Milly," he said.

"Oh, is she a new person who lives at your house?"

"Yeah, and she hates Tinker Bell," Mac pointed to a cat in his picture, cowering under a bush. The cat was so small that the teacher hadn't seen it.

"Oh, it looks frightened."

"She kicks it," he said.

"Mack," she said, "are you scared of Milly too?"

"Yeah, cause she hurts Tinker Bell if I do something bad."

"That sounds so sad, Mack." As she said this, he became red in the face and pushed back tears. "Let's go talk to someone who can help with this, okay?" she asked. When he nodded, she took him to a more private area at the vice principal's office, where the school counselor met them.

Mack's teacher knew that since animals were being abused at home, Mack was at higher risk for being abused too. Mack was living with emotional trauma every day with his new "step" parent. The teacher wisely found a trauma-informed interviewer to take it from there, and later in the day the vice principal took steps to file an abuse report to the department of human services.

Mack's father's new girlfriend was, in fact, abusing Mack by using threats to the cat and intimidation. She had hit him on more than one occasion, and his long-sleeved shirts covered up burn marks she had inflicted on his arms. A subsequent medical examination found that he also had burn marks on his genitals.

When parents abandon a child, it takes a lifetime for the child to develop trust again. Mack lost his biological mother and gained a dangerous bully. Mack lost his sister's protection too, as she had been the person he could always confide in. Mack's father was not a safe person for Mack, since he unwisely brought another "mother" figure into their home way too quickly. His father was wrapped up in his work and full of anger toward his ex-wife. Every time his father became angry, he raged about Mack's mother: "She doesn't care about you or me, Mack," he'd say. "She just wants my money." This alienation cut right into Mack's soul. He suddenly had no safe attachment.

I met Mack as his therapist when he was in his thirties. He'd had a series of failed relationships and also moved from job to job without a clear sense of direction. Since Mack's brain had been hardwired for fear at such a young age, he still responded to threats with strong physical and emotional reactions. He had a hard time separating out the signals his body sent to him and tried unsuccessfully to meet his attachment needs through sex. Several girlfriends left him because he randomly engaged in hookups with women he found online. His sexual behavior included painful stimuli, because he had come to associate pain with arousal. He seemed unable to find equilibrium, to calm down when needed, or to plan and execute his own goals. He was unable to tell safe activities and behaviors from self-harming behaviors. He had a hard time understanding that his life choices were driven by his trauma experiences (lodged in his hind brain) rather than well thought-out plans and analysis (available in the frontal cortex). This was all a direct physiological consequence of his childhood trauma.

In his book *The Body Keeps the Score*, Bessel van der Kolk describes what was going on inside Mack's brain as he struggled.

> The rational brain is primarily concerned with the world outside us: understanding how things and people work and figuring out how to accomplish our goals, manage our time, and sequence our actions. Beneath the rational brain lie two evolutionarily older, and to some degree separate, brains, which are in charge of everything else: the moment-by-moment registration and management of our body's physiology and the identification of comfort, safety, threat, hunger, fatigue, desire, longing, excitement, pleasure, and pain.[3]

Put simply, Mack had an underdeveloped forebrain, and he needed time to develop and practice using it. The system in his brain called

> When parents abandon a child, it takes a lifetime for the child to develop trust again.

"executive function" had shut down during and after his trauma. He compensated by responding from that primitive, lower brain (sometimes called the reptilian brain). Many trauma survivors find themselves reacting emotionally before they engage their thinking and planning functions. Van der Kolk referred to the first growth in developing frontal lobe capability as the "first grade." These capacities were disrupted for Mack when he was, in fact, in the first grade. As an adult he had to backtrack to learn those missing skills. Once he could sit still, use his words, understand abstract concepts, make plans, and attune to the people around him, he could move toward more complex skills.[4] In therapy Mack learned mindfulness to slow down his reactive emotions, to make plans and implement them, and to consider the consequences for his actions.

> Mindfulness is a therapeutic technique to raise awareness of the present moment. It helps survivors to observe and accept their thoughts, feelings, and bodily sensations.

Mack had to rethink his efforts to find a loving partner. He clearly had reason enough to lack trust in himself or others. His mistrust was a safe strategy that backfired when he wanted a partner and longed for trusted attachment. He learned that while he had been trying to make sex do the job of love, he had actually been abandoning himself in the way he had been abandoned by his parents during childhood. Many trauma survivors abandon themselves. Recognizing this was a huge "ahah!" moment in therapy. Mack found the capacity to heal and made good use of therapy to become conscious about and end his self-destructive patterns.

> He had been trying to make sex do the job of love.

Stolen Sexuality

Patricia's father snuck into her room every night for seven years. "What's even worse," she said, "is that I know my mother would have noticed him missing beside her." Her voice grew stronger and louder as she asked rhetorical questions to convey her total outrage. "She never followed him? Never asked him where he'd been?" She was red in the face and her hands began trembling. "My father abused me, and my mother allowed it, like the guard in prison watching a fellow guard bludgeon an inmate with his nightstick. Maybe she was relieved that he wasn't forcing her to do it. I don't know. None of it is any excuse for what they did to me."

I nodded and said, "You didn't deserve their abuse."

She sat back on the couch in my counseling office and shed the tears she'd held back for over thirty years.

How can I describe the insidiousness of child sexual abuse? Our culture minimizes child sexual abuse and mistakenly thinks children are so resilient they can easily overcome it. We downplay abuse with absurd statements such as, "Men need to have their sexual needs met." Ellen Bass and Laura Davis's widely read book, *The Courage to Heal: A Guide for Women Survivors of Child Sexual Abuse*, begins with a list describing many types of abuse.[5] They needed to include the list because in 1988, when Harper and Row first published the book, sexual abuse was so culturally normalized that many trauma survivors didn't consciously "know" they had been abused. Since perpetrators describe their behaviors as "education," "doing something nice for each other," and so on, victims often have no firm ground upon which to understand their later symptoms like hypervigilance, sex avoidance, unusual physical pain, and distrust in interpersonal relationships.

When *The Courage to Heal* was published, few people equated sexual abuse with power and violence, and for centuries mothers have been shrugging their shoulders and telling their daughters it's just what girls go through. When Sigmund Freud first documented and published data saying that his patients had been sexually abused by their wealthy aristocratic fathers, the people who funded his research threatened to shut him down if he didn't recant. It was then that he formulated his theory that these girls had not been abused but were simply fantasizing, due to their affectionate desires for their fathers. I'd like to say that people have moved beyond blaming victims for their perpetrators' predatory sexuality, but we still have a long way to go.

Since culture has been extremely slow to recognize child sexual abuse trauma's lasting impacts, I am including definitions of sexual abuse in the nearby sidebar. For readers who have had these experiences, a word of caution. You may not have considered

> Our culture minimizes child sexual abuse and mistakenly thinks children are so resilient they can easily overcome it.

> I'd like to say that people have moved beyond blaming victims for their perpetrators' predatory sexuality, but we still have a long way to go.

your experience as abuse, and you may not agree that you were traumatized by something on this list. It's not easy to tell whether you have minimized your experience in order to cope with it or have worked your way through it to be healed. You are the only one who can decide that. As I said previously, not everyone with similar trauma wounds feels the impact the same way. If you read through this list and find that you are now ready to name your experience and safely address it, though, I urge you to find a therapist to help you along the way.

In all of these circumstances, coercion is present, though it may not always seem like coercion. I have a male friend who learned about sexuality from a woman fifteen years older than he was. He didn't define what happened to him as abuse; he saw it as early education to help him become a better lover later in life. She pitched it to him that way to get him to participate. He still thinks about sex with her as "love" to protect himself from the feelings of powerless vulnerability that come with being a victim.

Children don't willingly participate in adult-to-child sexual acts. They have no ability to give consent. The child has no power, and the perpetrator has full power to engage in or stop behavior. The child's body may respond as it has been created to respond when sexually engaged, but this in no way indicates willing participation. When adults prey upon a child's innate physiological responsiveness, the child is not giving consent. The adult is perpetrating trauma-inflicting abuse. Many victims suffer deep shame because they

Common Forms of Sexual Abuse

Sexual abuse includes being subjected to unnecessary medical treatments to satisfy an adult's sexual appetite; being forced to watch or listen to sexual material; being made to pose for photographs, videos, or films; being coerced into participation in pornography; being vaginally or anally penetrated (raped); being stroked, kissed, or entrapped for adult sexual gratification; being tortured as part of ritualized abuse; being made to watch a live sexual act or pornography; and being forced to perform oral sex on an adult or sibling.

became aroused during their abuse, even though the context for this sexual response was badly distorted.

Sexual abuse is about power and intimidation. Incest inflicts fear and calls it love. Perpetrators convince their young prey that they are "special" and that they are just being asked to respond with love and affection. Sexual abuse often includes weeks and months of grooming before physical contact is made. Confusing attention with love, victims have a hard time sorting these adult behaviors out prior to abuse, during abuse, and decades thereafter.

Sexual abuse trauma is more insidious than other trauma wounds. When fear and terror overtake victims during car crashes or school shootings, afterward they find ways to avoid those locations. Along the side of the road, makeshift flowers and crosses memorialize places where loved ones died. Schools close down rooms and hallways and never reopen them again or transform them into permanent memorials. Soldiers returning from war can be physically far away from the places where pain and horror occurred. For incest victims the trauma took place in and on their bodies, including very private areas such as breasts, buttocks, and genitals. How do they get away from those places? And how do they avoid those places if they wish to have a sexual life as an adult?

> **When adults prey upon a child's innate physiological responsiveness, the child is not giving consent. The adult is perpetrating trauma-inflicting abuse.**
>
> **Incest inflicts fear and calls it love.**

Grooming behaviors may include:

- Special attention, outings, extra privileges, and gifts
- Isolating a child from others
- Excessively flattering a child
- Filling a child's unmet needs
- Becoming "family" to a child
- Treating a child as if he or she is older
- Gradually crossing physical boundaries, and becoming increasingly intimate/sexual
- Use of secrecy, blame/shame, and threats to maintain control[6]

Child sexual abuse survivors face their hormones jump-started at earlier ages than their peers. This leads many survivors into early sexual behaviors and sexual partner seeking. Victims may repeat their abuse scenarios as victims or as abusers. And their desire for sex can either be quite strong or the exact opposite, nonexistent. Some survivors avoid the "scene of the crime" altogether. I've met with sexual trauma victims who have a hard time bathing or showering because they can't even touch themselves "down there," since they still feel "dirty." Others avoid preventative annual examinations and fail to seek treatment for genital illnesses.

The avoidance of sexual behaviors or their own genitalia keeps abuse victims from experiencing anxiety-producing flashbacks, nightmares, and panic. Since arousal and fear normally run on the same channel in the brain, a fear response during sex can either increase arousal or shut down sexual response. Many victim/survivors have the frustrating experience of wanting sexual connection and finding that they shut down instantly when they become frightened. Their sexual attraction and arousal are suppressed, so that safety can be assured. This frustrating experience keeps them from fully enjoying their own sexuality and fully enjoying sex with a partner.

Child Sex Abuse in the Church "Family"

Abuse victims are heaped with shame during and following their abuse. Churchgoing victims feel deeply ashamed when they hear preachers use language like promiscuity, fornication, and sodomy. Since they most often presume that their abuse is or was their fault, these messages about sexual sin plunge them into silence and secrecy. Take a minute to imagine yourself at church on a Sunday morning, knowing that your brother had forced you into sexual behavior the night before. Then you hear the preacher say that girls must be "unblemished" virgins who save themselves for marriage. You would feel doubly doomed.

Children with sexual abuse trauma grow into adolescence thinking that they are unworthy of finding love because they are already "tainted" or "damaged goods." These messages are reinforced by abusers and by adults and parents when victims tell the truth about their abuse. They are left with internal shame and then emotionally condemned by systemic family shame.

There is a correlation between physical, mental, or sexual abuse at home and child sexual abuse at church. Vulnerable youth who are neglected or abused at home find their way to churches in search of reparative families. A teen boy who was abused by his youth director was told repeatedly by his mother that he should make friends with the minister. She was looking for a better father figure for her boy than his own alcoholic, "good for nothing" father at home. The deal sounded good to him too. At first. Until the sexual abuse began.

Jolanda's Story

Jolanda went to church with her mother and father every Wednesday night and every Sunday. The church was her "home away from home." Her mother worked two jobs, and her father's railroad job kept him away from home for days at a time. In her freshman year the church started an after-school youth program that seemed to be a safe place. Her parents enrolled her in the program, relieved that she'd be well cared for among friends at the church instead of being home alone.

The assistant pastor at the church supervised volunteers who helped students with their homework and sports activities. Pastor Roland was in his mid-twenties, and he had graduated from Bible college the year before. He was always nice, and then *extra* nice, to Jolanda. After a few weeks in the program, he shooed away volunteers and helped her himself. She liked his attention, and she was happy to report about it at home. Her mother praised her for being "so special," and so did Roland. Roland started inviting her into his office to help her with her school work, and the two of them swapped jokes. He brought her sweet snacks and asked her not to tell anyone. He tacked her drawings up on his bulletin board.

Then one day, he put on music they could dance to, and during a slow song slipped his hand down the back of her pants. She felt confused but didn't stop him. The following week he read her some Bible verses about love and suggested that they wash each other's feet, the way Jesus did. Before long, he was also asking her to wash his genitals and masturbating in front of her—all the while asking for her to keep the encounters secret because they had a holy connection that no one else could understand. If she told anyone, he would say that she had invited his behavior, and she would be kicked out of the program.

She endured his sexual abuse for more than a year without speaking a word about it. She tried to stay out in the common areas as much as possible, but he continued to expose himself and demand touching when he got her alone. She finally got up the courage to say something to her mother, though she downplayed the full extent of his behavior. She said she didn't want to go to the program anymore. "He just gives me the creeps," she said. Her mother became angry.

"What am I supposed to do, then, Jolanda? Quit my job?"

"I don't know, Mom. Maybe I could find an after-school baby-sitting job."

"You don't have any experience with babies, honey. Who's going to hire you?"

"Mom, I could stay in the library after school."

This conversation went on for a long while, and Jolanda capitulated to her mother's desire that she stay in the program. But she didn't go to the church, instead she spent her after-school hours at school or walking the streets. Roland called Jolanda's home one evening to talk to her mother. He said she had not come in a while, that he missed her and wondered how she was doing. He was fishing to see if she had told her mother what had been going on.

"Have you pulled Jolanda out of the program?" he asked.

But Jolanda's mother did not know what he had been doing to her daughter and planned to confront Jolanda about her absences.

"I'll be letting her know that you called," her mother said.

He said, "I hope you will encourage her to return."

An unsupportive family environment left Jolanda stranded during the months her pastor abused her. She had no safe place for disclosure. It would take years of growing maturity for Jolanda to make the connections between her religious upbringing, which taught her to sacrifice herself for others, and her silent protection of her mother and her pastor during this ordeal.

Extreme Powerlessness

As I write this story I find my stomach churning and my heart rate increasing. I am starting to notice my own anger adrenaline rising. Reading this section, you may also find yourself feeling powerless and fearing the worst for her. You may have had a similar experience to Jolanda's—being trapped in sexual abuse, sworn to silence, and totally unable to find an advocate to help you. Or you may know a woman or man who was sexually abused by a parent, pastor, or priest.

I don't know how this story ends. Does Jolanda tell her schoolteacher? Does the schoolteacher report the abuse to the Department of Human Services? Does she tell her mother more and face her mother's shame or disbelief? Does her mother tell the senior pastor? And does he say, "I'll take care of the problem" but cover it up instead? Sadly, Jolanda's chances of being victimized yet again by those who disbelieve her, blame her, or make it all her fault are quite high.

Beyond Powerlessness

Where do victims begin to find and claim power? If Jolanda had even once told Roland "no" and stopped his abuse, she would have learned that she was powerful. If she had refused to go back to the program and suffered consequences, she would know at least, that she could use her power. If she had acted out or acted badly, she would have still been claiming her power. Yet none of these options were reasonable at the time. Years later she could find and use her power by telling the truth. She could claim her right to justice by filing lawsuits within the church or in civil court. By finding and joining a support group with other survivors, Jolanda could hasten her healing process. She could tell her story in a post on #metoo.[7]

There are other powers she could claim that would lead her toward healing. She could learn to control her post-traumatic stress symptoms. She could learn to manage her emotions and claim the sexuality she wants rather than the sexuality she was forced to experience. She could find the power to forgive herself and offer herself grace for the behaviors she couldn't have stopped when she was in Roland's office all those years ago. By reaching out for help, Jolanda could find resurrection power.

Reclaiming Sexuality

Sexual abuse victims, like other trauma victims, are healed by various therapy techniques, speaking out, supportive friends and partners, faith exploration, and sometimes sheer willpower. These will be more explicitly spelled out later in the book. In this section I want to focus on strategies to heal victims' sexual lives, because self-help books have tended to avoid this part in the healing process. Sexual abuse victims have to learn ways to reclaim their own bodies.

Craig had been sexually abused as a pre-teen, and he was married and had young adult children by the time he was ready to face his trauma wounds. Craig had always engaged in flirtatious behaviors with women, and since he was charming, handsome, and held an impressive position within his company, he found them responsive. He typically stopped building intimacy with women just shy of sex with them. But he liked their attention and the sense of power he felt when he believed that they would be available if he only asked. And then, he crossed over his own line and had an affair. This behavior reinforced his shame, cut across everything he believed he was supposed to be as a Christian man, and made him face his deepest fears and his past.

Knowing that his wife would leave him if he told her, he called me so that he could see a therapist with whom he could keep his secret, at least until he was fully ready to tell the truth. His sex life with his wife had always been good, but after the affair he couldn't maintain an erection. (Our genitals are very honest during emotional and relational experiences.) The more he explored this condition the more he was able to see the connection between his childhood abuse and his power and control over women. Feeling powerless as a child victim, he flipped that feeling over and made victims of others—including the women he flirted with, his wife, and himself. He was trying to regain his lost power. And in truth, he was angry at his own penis for wanting so much and behaving so badly. Healing required that he take a look at his emotional and physical impotence as the toll that trauma had taken years before.

I asked Craig to write a letter to the cousin who had abused him in childhood and not send it but use the process for growth. I asked him to describe his feelings during the abuse, to empathize with his child-self, and to say anything that he felt. The process seemed daunting, so I also asked him to stop at any time if putting the truth on paper became overwhelming. The next week at session he had completed the letter, and by reading it aloud, he began to tell me the heartrending story about his trauma wounds. As his past made more sense to him, so did his body's responses and his behaviors. He saw his behaviors in context rather than isolation. And at home, he found his sex life returning, with much less shame.

His healing eventually involved telling his wife about the affair, and they entered therapy together. She despised him for his behavior, but when they both explored its symbolic meaning and connection to his abuse, they could see it for what it was and move forward to restore trust in the marriage. Her grace significantly healed his shame.

> Our genitals are very honest during emotional and relational experiences.

Love Letters

When abuse survivors face internalized shame and physical self-loathing, I ask them to write love letters. The first letter is a love letter to their body. For example, a survivor might write,

> Dear Body,
>
> I am so sorry for what you went through. You felt so much pain, and you were so alone. I'm sorry I couldn't protect you from abuse. I was young, and I couldn't see a way to stop it. I know it left you feeling ugly and dirty. You just wanted it to stop, and sometimes you still feel the abuse, like an old scar that aches when it rains. I want to thank you for all that you can still do for me, for your strength and ways you help me move every day. I want to help you feel whole again, beautiful again, and sensual again. I promise to stop saying negative things to you, to feed you well, to offer you exercise and good sleep, and help you to know that you are an amazing body.
>
> Love,
>
> Me

The second letter I assign the client is a response from his/her/their body. It's wonderful to see how the body knows what it needs and what to ask for. For victims who put on a good deal of weight to protect themselves from sexual feelings or being "sexy" to others, this is a very powerful exercise. For victims who have abused their bodies by cutting or by drug and alcohol consumption, this dialogue can lead to alternative strategies when overwhelming memories and feelings arise. When victims have survived by turning against their bodies, this reconciliation is necessary.

The Partner's Role

Trauma survivors often enter into sex, even with safe and supportive partners, in a disconnected way. They may dissociate in order to avoid triggers to sexually traumatizing events and memories. Sex becomes rote and unfulfilling. Sex therapists teach individuals and couples to avoid the problem known as *spectatoring*—remaining mentally observant during every movement in their sexual choreography, which shuts down their ability to experience sex sensually. Many arousal and orgasmic disorders come from spectatoring. It's totally understandable that people who were harmed during sex may avoid their feelings by playing the role of observer rather than engaging as a full participant. It keeps their terror from resurfacing.

To heal, willing partners must slow down and remain in emotional contact throughout the arousal and orgasmic experience. Partners of abuse victims need to let their partners set the pace for sex and let them say "no" to *any* sexual behavior at *any* time. Often the victim/survivor needs to take charge during sex and talk about any triggers that arise. When a movement or position triggers old memories or fear, they both need to stop the behavior and return to holding and cuddling. Being held when scared, as I've said, lowers the fear circuitry in the brain and increases confidence and trust. Child abuse recovery expert Laura Davis has a good book to help partners develop compassion and sensitivity that helps victims become survivors in life and in the bedroom.[8]

With a safe, patient, and understanding partner, abuse survivors can rewire the brain's circuitry to lower fear and increase arousal. Recovery from sexual abuse trauma includes conscious choice-making about sexual behavior, self-forgiveness for what many survivors call "having been there" (even though they could not have escaped), and reclaiming their body's sacredness.

A safe sexual partner can help a victim regain the innocence and playfulness within sexuality that was horribly distorted during childhood. Couples therapists can generally teach partners to help their trauma-wounded lovers. For example, a couple can identify positions and activities that were once forced upon the victim and learn to avoid those triggers. They can then claim new positions and activities that awaken positive feelings. They can, in a sense, go back to the innocence of new and sacred sexuality one careful step at a time.

> Partners of abuse victims need to let their partners set the pace for sex and let them say "no" to *any* sexual behavior at *any* time.

A Final Note to Survivors

Fears about sexuality are common for everyone, and they need not limit your ability to reclaim a sex life of your choosing. When you find ways to love your body, you can begin to bring healthy sexuality back into your life. Beginning with sensate focus—a mindfulness practice that teaches you to put your thoughts on hold so that your senses can awaken—you may begin to notice the good things your body feels and does. Once you have left behind your fears and learned to stop intrusive memories from taking over in the bedroom you can learn safe and satisfying sexual techniques.[9]

If you are single, you may choose to remain free from partner sex. You may also choose to live without sensual touch or orgasms. Or, you may want to develop sexual experiences on your own through sex toys and masturbation. Becoming acquainted with your own body, and loving your own body, can free you from the shame that binds you to the past.

Becoming familiar with your body's sexual response cycle is a lifelong process. So start slowly to avoid shame-triggering experiences. Avoid watching pornography, because this could exacerbate trauma symptoms and increase shame. You don't need to compare yourself to an adult film star, nor expect yourself to look like or behave like one. If you want to learn about healthy sexuality, take a college course, or buy a college textbook. But more importantly, learn sexuality by learning to know and appreciate *your* unique and wonderful body. You have an awesome body. Put that on a sticky note on your bathroom mirror, and read it aloud every day until you believe it.

Hearing many stories from victim/survivors inclines me to end this chapter with appreciation for their courageous truth-telling. For Briana, Mack, Jolanda, Craig, and all child sexual abuse survivors who face their darkest secrets, I give them back the honor they once had stolen from them and so greatly deserve. As Rita Nakashima Brock said, "Remembering violence requires a descent into hell."[10]

And yet survivors walk there willingly when loneliness becomes too great, they get stuck in unsatisfying relationships, or they decide to reclaim the sacredness of their bodies. After the descent, the way out becomes clearer.

New people who learn I'm a psychologist ask how I can work with people who have been violated and abused. "Isn't it depressing?" is a comment I'm repeatedly asked. My answer is this. "I am so greatly blessed by the chance to witness transformation and resurrection that the walk into darkness is worth it."

For Reflection and Discussion

1 Why do you think that being *different* in a family leads to being targeted for abuse?

2 Has someone close to you been a victim of sexual assault? What was it like to learn this, and how did you respond?

3 Describe a few necessary steps sex abuse victims take during recovery.

4 What can you (and your faith community) do to prevent child sexual abuse?

6

When Uprooted: Immigration Heartbreak

I pulled my car over to park along a dozen tan stucco apartments built in the 1960s that looked as if they had not been painted for the twenty-five intervening years. The windows in most units were open and colorful curtains fluttered out gaps in broken screens. I walked up a cracked paved driveway looking for building number six. The grassy areas that used to surround these buildings were gone, but the dirt was not neglected or trashed. Every bit of land had been turned into vegetable gardens. Rows and rows of bamboo-poles supported corn and climbing cucumbers in raised beds, and squash bulged over their furrowed mounds.

Once I found the apartment building where my parishioners were living, a door cracked open. The wife in the household peeked out to see who it was, and then I was generously welcomed in. She pointed to the shoe mat where I placed my shoes and we went to the main space in the house and sat on small pillows on the floor. Soon her husband arrived, and she offered us tea, then went around the corner to prepare it. As was their custom, she hovered around the edges but did not join our conversation.

The Xiong family was among the many Lao Hmong refugees who resettled in the United States after the invasion of Laos and at the end of the Vietnam War. They were granted refugee status (though not without lengthy congressional debate) due to human rights violations they had suffered. Because they assisted US soldiers during the war, they were imprisoned, tortured, and killed. Many fled for their lives.

The Xiong family left nearly everything behind and fled on foot across North Vietnam to reach a refugee resettlement camp across the Mekong River, and lived in Thailand before being granted asylum. Mr. Xiong told me that his elderly father started out on the journey with him, his wife, and their young children.

He bowed toward me and stood up. "I'll be right back," he said. He returned with a small wooden box and put it between us on the floor. He carefully opened the hinged lid in my direction.

The next few minutes in this story feel very private to me, and I hope that setting it down on paper doesn't diminish the incredible trust he had in me as he lifted the lid to his box. I saw a folded brilliant blue cloth, similar to scarves I saw Hmong families use to transport food dishes and daily household goods. He lifted it out and set it aside on the floor near his knee. Beneath it was a dented silver cup with a well-worn handle, the only drinking vessel the family used for weeks. He carefully set it on the rug between us, and the area was transformed into an altar.

Also from the box, he pulled out a small picture of his parents and he leaned it against the cup where I could see it. His father's death along the route contributed to his Christian conversion. When his father became very sick on the journey, they knocked on the doors of strangers to find help. Many households turned them away (fearing illness and the very bad fortune of having someone die in their home), but a Christian family took his dying father in and eased his suffering. After he died they let the Xiong family stay for mourning rituals.

Mr. Xiong's next reach into the box brought forth a worn and yellowed folded envelope. He raised the flap on it and shook it out, smiling. Nothing fell out. I smiled back—he had played a funny trick on me. "Seeds," he said. "They are . . ." He pointed out the door and window to the surrounding gardens. From my Western viewpoint, if I ever had to flee for my life, I doubt I'd have thought about seeds. But the Xiong family farmed the land in northern Laos, and seeds were life for them, both food to eat, and enough to sell to others. Having seeds, they believed, they could start over again. Those were seeds of hope.

> Among refugees and asylum-seekers, trauma includes three stages: the trauma before refugee status and asylum are granted, adjustments during resettlement, and personal and social identity formation afterward.

And then he showed me a few coins at the bottom of the box and laid them on the altar rug too. He grew very silent for a while. "We ran and ran," he said, "in danger, all the time, danger." He draped the blue fabric over his shoulders and hunched forward for a few moments, holding onto the ends and I could see that it was a hand-sewn backpack. He grew still, catching an insufficient breath. And I don't recall his words exactly. I will not diminish this moment with him by putting his experience into my own words. What I learned that day is this: while he and his family were on the run they were crossing through a large overgrown field when they encountered bursts of gunfire. Terrified, they ran for cover. Mr. Xiong had his two-year-old baby in the blue pack on his back. A bullet pierced through the fabric and killed her instantly.

When he finished telling me this, we were both silent as he pushed back terror and tears. He removed the cloth from his back and showed me the hole in the fabric. Then he slowly folded the cloth and patted it. Placing everything back into the box, he wiped his eyes with the back of his hand and lifted it up as a pastor lifts the communion bread or holds up a newly baptized baby. He said, "This is—my box of tears."

THE XIONG family, like other refugees, came to the US with overwhelming PTSD, which was made worse by the less-than-warm welcome they received.[1] In many resettlement areas, apartments where Hmong families lived were regularly vandalized. In our town, cars parked on the streets were often broken into—their tires slashed; neighbors called the police about insignificant annoyances, and racial slurs were hurled at them. Community members, mistaking them for the North Vietnamese we had fought against in

> Among refugees and asylum-seekers, trauma includes three stages: the trauma before refugee status and asylum are granted, adjustments during resettlement, and personal and social identity formation afterward. It is difficult to assess and treat the trauma carried by immigrants within traumatized communities. Refugees and asylum seekers have undergone so many traumatic experiences that typical psychological trauma scales cannot be used to measure them.

the war, harassed them and refused to hire them. For these families, a hard work ethic, rock-solid Christian beliefs, and the desire for education helped them to overcome obstacles. In our area, they had a church, and a Hmong pastor who was appointed to serve them.

From Saint Paul, Minnesota, to Fresno, California, Southeast Asian communities recreated the loyalty bonds and support they had experienced before the war back home. But the trauma toll was also evident among them. Gangs emerged in urban and suburban communities, food insecurity was common, language barriers prevented good healthcare, and work discrimination remained highly problematic. These factors interfered with their ability to take necessary steps in emotional recovery. While people are busy trying to meet their most basic needs, they can't afford to slow down and feel feelings. Therapy and emotional support groups can help trauma survivors, but many survivors lack the privilege or social status to access them.

Opportunities for Refugee Ministries Today

The United Nations High Commissioner's 2016 Report on Refugees revealed 21.3 million refugees worldwide. More than 3.3 million (15.5 percent) have been resettled in the United States since 1975.[2] Many refugees still leave their homelands because they are no longer safe in them. They arrive with trauma after having been persecuted for their nationality, race, religion, or political activity. Many are noncombatant victims in war. They have experienced such horrors in their home countries that they, like the Xiong family, risk their lives to flee. They walk for days, are caught in crossfire and shot at, watch people die, suffer hunger and illness. Some of them are forced to kill someone or be killed themselves. Others are conscripted into gang warfare that requires them to commit or witness horrendously violent acts.

Upon arrival in the United States, these refugees are not typically screened for mental health issues, including either current or past trauma. Mental health services lag behind in providing for their

> According to Jason Ostrander at Sacred Heart University in Fairfield, Connecticut, many refugees are "forced into migration and resettlement due to exposure to violence and/or other traumas in their home country, including political violence, discrimination, child abuse, war, human trafficking or other human rights violations. Refugees report high rates of torture, including witnessing torture of family members or others, physical beating, rape/sexual assault, and deprivation of food and water."[3]

needs. Insurance companies have been slow to pay for interpreters to assist refugee and asylum seekers during mental health treatment. Children in immigrant families (who pick up English quickly at school) often become language interpreters for the whole family. Therapists, social workers, clergy and lay ministers can help trauma-exposed immigrants by advocating for culturally sensitive healthcare and mental health services—including evaluation and treatment.

Faith communities across the US are responding to present-day challenges immigrants face, such as increases in deportations, and many are taking action by sheltering undocumented immigrants. In small towns and rural areas where culturally sensitive mental health services are not available, clergy and congregations frequently step in without adequate training, increasing the likelihood that these advocates will develop secondary trauma symptoms. Caring individuals nevertheless shelter mothers with children, extended families, and individuals separated from loved ones. They assist with driving, language tutoring, women's health issues, filling out paperwork, and providing childcare—greatly easing fears and burdens.

From acts of kindness and hospitality, to outright defiance as US policies tighten and limit immigration, many congregations and clergy stand alongside immigrants and asylum seekers who are being retraumatized by systemic injustice. A man who has lived and worked in the US for the past twenty years applied for citizenship more than a year ago. Meanwhile tension and fear remain constant. His lawyer informed him that the backlog in our state is more than eight hundred cases. "In this climate," the lawyer said, "it's best not to call attention to yourself for any reason." A faith community waits with him and prays with him.

The anxiety hundreds of families experience while their paperwork sits on top of someone's desk adds to fatigue, sleeplessness, and despair—conditions leading to depression. The children of illegal immigrants and asylum seekers who were born and raised in the US had a level of certainty about their status under the previous administration. They are now daily dosed with stress and uncertainty. Low-level anxiety is as trauma-inducing as a single incident and can be even more detrimental to overall health.

At the Border—Separations and Fear Interviews

When families arrive at US borders, they are no longer certain they will ever see each other again. While immigration policies change rapidly (even as I write this book), the uncertainty and fear at our borders continues. The policy of separating families at the border and during detention has led many people to question the moral compass of our nation. After suffering multiple traumas before arriving in the United States, the very real possibility exists that family members may temporarily or permanently be taken away from each other.

Children's attachment to parents cannot be severed without long-term psychological damage. Trauma specialist Bessel Van der Kolk told *Time* reporter Jamie Ducharme that children experience something like "psychological starvation" when separated. "Depriving them of their caregivers has effects on their brain as profound as starving them." He goes on to say that these children end up depressed and anxious and have long-term difficulty trusting others, regulating their emotions, and forming healthy relationships.[4]

News reports suggest that many minors, some of whom arrived on their own at the borders and some of whom were separated upon arrival, are now unaccounted for.[5]

> From acts of kindness and hospitality, to outright defiance as US policies tighten and limit immigration, many congregations and clergy stand alongside immigrants and asylum seekers who are being retraumatized by systemic injustice.

> The anxiety hundreds of families experience while their paperwork sits on top of someone's desk adds to fatigue, sleeplessness, and despair—conditions leading to depression.

Conditions for children in immigration and relocation centers vary, but many arrive or become sick, and a new strategy by immigration enforcers has been to separate children from their parents and force them to corroborate their parent's stories during interviews.

On the radio one morning, I heard news that the US government had decided to address the backlog in refugee and asylum applications by speeding up the process. That sounded like a good thing, but it was actually a public relations spin on a terrible new way to handle the flood of refugees into the US. News story sound bites made me think that most refugees crossing the US Mexico border are Mexicans seeking better jobs or dealing drugs. But due to Mexico's rising economy and increasing job availability, statistics show that immigration by Mexican citizens has decreased for the past fifteen years. Something else is actually happening.

Accounts about US illegal immigration often miss the real story—the increase in border crossings by asylum seekers from Central America, particularly Guatemala, El Salvador, and Honduras. These three countries have high murder rates, extensive crime due to cocaine trafficking, rape, and gangs that recruit and conscript locals through extortion and killing.[6]

Refugees and asylum seekers arrive at the US border with greater trauma levels than ever seen before. They need to be evaluated and helped, but instead, they are intimidated and interrogated at for-profit US processing centers. When refugees are put through immediate evaluation procedures, traumatized women and children lack the mental stability necessary to make a case for their asylum.

Although many women arrive with traumatic wounds from sexual violence, sex trafficking, spousal abuse, and gang recruitment, they are still being asked to recount their stories in a process called a "fear interview." In this interview an Immigration Services employee (usually male) sits with a woman and asks her to tell him why she is afraid to return home. Her trauma experience comes under scrutiny during an intensive interview with the terrifying possibility that she will be sent back into violence and trauma if she doesn't fully reveal her story or sufficiently demonstrate the danger.

Feelings of shame, fear of retaliation by active gangs for telling what happened to her, and fears that a male partner will reject and abandon her if her story is placed in a file are all deterrents to disclosure. During the interview she may reexperience the traumatic incident, become numb, silent, cry out, or curl in upon herself. Without a system that considers her traumatic symptoms, she can fail to pass the screening by remaining silent and appearing to be uncooperative during the most important conversation in her life.

Without a right to legal representation or a hearing before a judge, men, women, and children are too often returned across the border without assistance. These increasingly common quick evaluation processes, which anti-immigration proponents suggest are necessary to clean up the backlog of illegal criminals and drug dealers, adversely affect people with trauma. Being held at a detention center does not allow time for trauma symptoms to ease enough for people to tell their stories.

Immigration lawyers, who have been able to observe detention centers and hearings, say that "forcing traumatized mothers and their children to quickly undergo credible fear interviews in detention undermines [the] asylum officers' ability to accurately assess fear of return and may lead to erroneous deportations. . . . Disclosing traumatic events requires trust and a certain level of comfort that cannot be achieved in detention. Consequently, traumatized individuals may be deprived of due process and, ultimately, protection under U.S. law."[7] They are strongly urging that fast-track procedures be eliminated. Expedited immigration determinations are grossly inhumane to traumatized refugees and asylum seekers.

As I spelled out in an earlier chapter, any separation from loved ones creates a trauma legacy. For many refugee children, connections to loved ones have provided the only safety net they

> Expedited immigration determinations are grossly inhumane to traumatized refugees and asylum seekers.

have had in the midst of terrifying circumstances. When families arrive at our borders, a more compassionate process needs to be found to keep them together at arrival, in detention facilities, and during resettlement hearings. The practice of forced separations between parents and children in some Immigration and Customs Enforcement (ICE) branches in the "hope" that families will willingly leave the country (or refrain from trying to cross the border in the first place) has been challenged and hopefully ended. Christian communities are influencing immigration policies by circulating petitions, writing letters to agencies, and continuing to raise public awareness.

These efforts to stop family separations are not only helping current generations, they will have long-lasting effects. Research suggests that rises in circulating stress hormone levels during trauma change the human genome. Rachel Yehuda, a specialist in epigenetics and the intergenerational effects of trauma, said, "The descendants of people who survived the Holocaust have different stress hormone levels than their peers, perhaps predisposing them to anxiety disorders."[8] Increased cortisol availability helps the body cope under constant threat or prolonged starvation. Her studies show that mothers who had PTSD produced children with low levels of "cortisol-busting" enzymes, therefore higher cortisol levels, making them more likely to be symptomatic in fearful and high-stress situations. People whose brains are flooded by overwhelming fear will likely pass vulnerabilities down subsequent generations.[9]

The Hebrew scripture, in Exodus 20:4, says that the iniquity of the fathers will be visited "upon the children to the third and fourth generation." Trauma passes down in this way too. Generational

> Survivor studies by Dr. Rachel Yehuda, professor of psychiatry at the Icahn School of Medicine at Mount Sinai, suggest that the offspring of extremely traumatized people may be at high risk for PTSD.

trauma can be found among many US populations including African Americans, Native Americans, and Central American asylum seekers.

Acculturation in a Strange Land

When immigrant families begin anew in the US, even under the best of circumstances their awareness of being different is in and of itself traumatizing. Relocated away from extended family, religious rituals and traditions, and friends they feel at ease with, most immigrant children face bullying and put up emotional walls. After an incident at school where she was bullied, Rita Nakashima Brock coped by placing a "shield" around her pain.[10] Rita's Japanese mother met and married an American soldier who was stationed overseas during the war. She writes, "Being Japanese made me a target of inexplicable hostility in America, the pain of which I hid behind a shield of invulnerability, which I thought of as my American self, the part of me that acted confident and impermeable."[11]

For decades immigration laws made a high priority of family reunification, which enhances mental health for everyone in the family system. First-degree relatives were high on priority lists for immigration. These policies are based on sound psychological research into attachment as a key element in trauma healing. Having an extended family makes a crucial difference in mental health outcomes for resettled children.

At the university where I teach, many young immigrants face uncertainty and grief on a daily basis. They talk about food and housing insecurity and daily face both subtle and overt racist aggression on campus. They carry unseen grief and loneliness to school with them every day.

Author and theologian Rita Nakashima Brock beautifully writes about her immigration experience, with universal themes:

> Like so many Americans, I have had to reconstruct my life, to make myself anew. Dislocation, the aftermath of violence, trauma, and isolation reach back for generations among American families. Americans have lost languages and lands and lives. Genocide and forced relocation, kidnapping and enslavement, immigration, the need to take refuge from poverty, war, and terrorism, illicit border crossings or sea voyages have disrupted our ancestral legacies. . . . We are like the ancient Israelites trying to find a home in the wilderness, unable to go back, uncertain of where we wander.[12]

In every place and time, as wars have scarred the earth and the people on it, refugees have fled in fear and sought safety in foreign lands. Almost everyone in the Bible was dislocated or crossed territorial and race boundaries, beginning with Adam and Eve's banishment from Eden. In the Noah story both animals and humans are relocated. When violence erupted between Cain and Abel, the killer was protected by exile. Moses was an immigrant shamed for marrying outside his race. There are kings on the list who go to battle, conquer lands, and leave a wake of refugees behind them. Abraham and Sarah go out to search for promised land. An unexpected former sex worker (or perhaps not), Rahab worked in counterintelligence in a foreign land during a war. She's on that list of saints in the book of Hebrews, as are many, many immigrant refugees and asylum seekers. The scripture says, "They confessed that they were strangers and foreigners on the earth" (Heb 11:13).

A pastoral colleague came to visit last week wearing a shirt that says, "Jesus was an immigrant." It startled me at first, but it makes total sense. Jesus was born far from home, and when Herod's infant-killing spree threatened his life, his family was uprooted again. Using the valuable gifts brought to them by foreign Magi, they had enough money to cross over into Egypt. His family left behind everyone they had known including Mary's helpful mentor, her aunt Elizabeth. They took little with them. They spoke a different language and were used to different customs (Matt 2:13–15, 19–20). When it was safe to return home to Nazareth, they made another journey and readjusted.

Jesus's call to ministry took him out to preach among strangers in Judea. His witness was met with resistance and constant threats of imprisonment. After all, "Can anything good come out of Nazareth?" (John 1:46). This ironic question points to the blindness we all have toward "outsiders," feeling threatened by perceived difference, while overlooking similarity.

We are all called, as Jesus was, to align ourselves with those who are wandering rather than with those who have settled, conquered, or amassed power and wealth. Who among us can claim that our ancestors have not been persecuted? In order to restore hope and foster healing, we need to say to the refugee and the asylum seeker, "We too are immigrants and strangers; come and live with us."

For Reflection and Discussion

1. Do you consider yourself an outsider within your culture or within the dominant culture? Why or why not?

2. Describe the racial and/or cultural diversity in your family and how different family members handle it.

3. Plan one action step to assist immigrant families in your community.

4. How might you enlist your faith community in response to current threats to deportees?

7

When Death Comes Suddenly: Gun Violence

> Thus says the Lord: A voice is heard in Ramah, lamentation and bitter weeping, Rachel is weeping for her children. She refuses to be comforted for her children because they are no more.
>
> —Jeremiah 31:15

FOURTEEN-YEAR-OLD JAMIE Guttenberg was among the seventeen students slain at Marjory Stoneman Douglas High School in South Florida in February 2018. Her father spoke at a memorial for his daughter, the school staff, and students. Expressing the shock and horror others were also feeling he said, "I don't know what I do next."[1] In a Facebook post he added, "I am broken as I write this, trying to figure out how my family gets through this."

When death comes suddenly through violence, words fail. Even the best speechwriters and politicians who make public statements after mass shootings fumble in their attempts at consolation. People who have not lost loved ones in this way barely grasp the horror and disorientation that these families go through for years after the day their loved one died. The experience is best summed up by Fred Guttenberg's seven words: "I don't know what to do next." Every predictable daily activity stops when a loved one is murdered. When the loved one is young, the family home becomes a shrine and a wailing wall; parents and siblings can barely comfort themselves while they try to comfort each other. A child's death rewrites the dependable order of aging and dying. Children are supposed to bury their parents, not the other way around. Nothing feels safe or predictable for days and months following sudden death.

I live where mountains create our landscape. When I try to express the emotional devastation parents go through with the loss of a child, I see it this way. Their emotional landscape is laid barren, as if a devastating wildfire had swept through and taken away all recognizable paths on which to travel. There is no road left, only scars and fallen trees. Nothing seems to be alive at all. The smoke fills the air for days, and everything is shrouded in falling embers. They really don't know what to do, and only other parents who have lost children fully know how to help them. Counselors, friends, and pastors can try to help, but many will blunder.

As pastor I made a home visit and sat with Marianne, who was new to the congregation. We sat across from each other in the room she called her "parlor." It was tastefully old-fashioned with brocade fabrics dominating the décor. Marianne sat in a chair that had perfectly molded itself around her for at least thirty years. In her early eighties, she had recently moved to our town to be near her only son, who promised to help her through—she laughed saying this—"my last days."

I asked if he was her only child. "Only one now," Marianne said, and she paused for a long while. She reached under the table nearby and drew out a photo album. The front pages were black-and-white wedding photos. "Meet my husband, Frank," she said. "He died young—I think that losing Susie broke his heart." She flipped a chunk of pages and stopped at a posed photograph from Sears at Christmas. "This is my son, Ronnie, and Frank and I, and this is Susie." Ronnie was nearly as tall as his father, and Susie looked to be nine or ten. I waited for her story without asking questions. I simply said, "Susie is beautiful."

"She was playing at a friend's house and the boy across the street accidentally dropped his gun and shot her." I caught myself barely breathing. "The accident happened the summer after this picture," she said. "Oh my, it's been more than fifty years."

As a well-meaning but naïve young pastor, I asked Marianne this question. "When did you get over it?" And then she became my teacher.

"Oh, my dear," she said with more kindness than I deserved, "you don't *get over* it."

> Nothing feels safe or predictable for days and months following sudden death.

Parents and Families Forever Changed

When children die, parents are forced to reorient themselves to a life they could not have anticipated and didn't want. A child's death from illness or cancer sometimes gives family members time to prepare for the loss and ways to talk about the loss before it happens. They have time to say goodbye. When sudden death disorients families, loved ones have a very different and much more traumatic experience. When they said, "Bye, . . . have a good day" or maybe "Love you, see you later," they didn't know they wouldn't see their child come back home at the end of the day. And if, on that particular day, they had been too busy or distracted to say much of anything, they will feel worse. And if, in the frustrations parents sometimes have, their last words were parental, "Go back to your room and get your coat," or slightly critical like, "Can't you figure this out by now—it's the middle of winter and you'll need your coat for heaven's sake," they will feel even worse. Maybe they didn't say anything at all as their child flew out the door and took off for school. On any given day, any parent would start the day thinking that tomorrow they'd get do-overs and hug days and a future in which to get it all right. And then they don't. And then they won't *get over it*.

Every student who dies suddenly has an extended family and a circle of friends who are thrust into a grief process. They all experience the world as unsafe and scramble for connections and security. Everyone at a school where a shooting takes place lives in fear for days, months, and sometimes years afterward.

A life-altering trauma also occurs for parents whose children are violently injured and survive. Those families have their lives reshaped as well. Many young gun-violence victims have permanent mental and physical disabilities the rest of their lives and need a level of care that families were not prepared for and that sometimes become financially devastating.

Far more students are exposed to gun violence than we might expect. A *Washington Post* analysis in February 2018 found that "more than 150,000 students attending at least 170 primary or secondary schools have experienced a shooting on campus since the Columbine High School massacre in 1999."[2] Students are also exposed to gun violence through the suicides of their peers, community violence, and homicides. Some of the students in these statistics have more than one trauma to contend with.

In fact, teenaged trauma victims face greater risks for developing a mental illness during recovery than their adult counterparts. When trauma comes at this time in life, teens are even more emotionally unprepared for the shock to the brain and body than the adults around them. They have less-developed frontal lobe capacities than people in early adulthood. Their emotional brains are in formative stages. The brain doesn't yet have a solid grasp on emotional regulation and may adapt to new anxiety states as if they were normal. The brain's ability to make new neuropathways makes it very adaptable and also very vulnerable to stress. Neurologist Frances E. Jensen, who along with Amy Ellis Nutt wrote the book *The Teenage Brain*, told *Time Magazine* that rapidly growing neuronal structures in a teenaged brain can negatively affect them even in normal circumstances. She says,

> About 70% of mental illnesses, including anxiety, mood and eating disorders, and psychosis, appear in the teen years and early adulthood. The timing makes sense, since the prefrontal cortex and frontal lobes are implicated in the emergence of diseases like depression and schizophrenia. Risks for health issues like addiction are also higher during this time period.[3]

When trauma wounds take place during these vulnerable years, teens have an increased risk for symptoms of mental illnesses and substance addictions. For example, the National Survey of Adolescents found that "teens who had experienced physical or sexual abuse/assault were three times more likely to report past or current substance abuse than those without a history of trauma. In

> When trauma comes at this time in life, teens are even more emotionally unprepared for the shock to the brain and body than the adults around them.

> **Statistics on Youth Gun Violence and Gun Access**
>
> - Firearm injuries are the cause of death of eighteen children and young adults (twenty-four years of age and under) each day in the US.
> - Children and young adults (twenty-four years of age and under) constitute 38 percent of all firearm deaths and nonfatal injuries.
> - In the United States, over 1.69 million kids age eighteen and under are living in households with loaded and unlocked firearms.
> - More than 75 percent of guns used in suicide attempts and unintentional injuries of zero- to nineteen-year-olds were stored in the residence of the victim, a relative, or a friend.[5]

surveys of adolescents receiving treatment for substance abuse, more than 70 percent of patients had a history of trauma exposure."[4]

While many teens show remarkable resilience, parents and educators need to be alert to symptoms of PTSD, depression, anxiety, and substance abuse following teens' exposure to a trauma. These risks vary across socioeconomic classes and ethnicities. Community support, survivor groups, and therapy can improve resilience. Trauma recovery for some will take several months; for others, years.

Life Disrupted

The gunfire changed everything. As parents, siblings, extended family members, and friends scramble to cope with violent death, they have two psychological processes going on simultaneously. They are going through stages of grief along with the process of trauma resolution. These grief stages were first identified by Elisabeth Kübler-Ross and include denial, anger, bargaining, depression, and acceptance.[6] She revised her theories over time and researchers have found that they are not always in the order she first suggested. The denial stage is sometimes called the stage of shock. Not everyone goes through every stage, and the stages can overlap.

News media interviews with teens after the Florida shooting found them naming their symptoms clearly. One boy was having dreams that the shooter was pointing a gun directly at his head. Another lay awake all night, staring at the wall, unable to sleep. These teens had intrusive memories about the moments when they were hiding in their classrooms or running in the halls. They had flashbacks that overtook them without notice. They lacked the ability to concentrate or complete school work. They were obsessed by news media reports. Acute trauma fully disrupted their lives.

Teen survivors who have moderate to severe symptoms after school shootings don't return to school. Others have their prior life goals entirely changed; they delay college and drop plans to move away from home. In Florida, students turned their grief into rage and launched a national youth movement to reduce access to guns and to eliminate bump stocks and automatic assault weapons.

Grieving siblings who lose a sister or brother to violence experience a passionate call to seek justice for their lost family member. They often find themselves making a commitment to succeed in life, as if they could achieve the life the lost sibling would have had. They may protect their parents by staying home or give up risk-taking physical activities because they are trying to keep their parents from facing another loss.

Bishop Minerva G. Carcaño, thirty-four years after her brother's death, published her family's story on a blog. She said, "My brother Paul was murdered. The death inflicting instrument was a gun. I lost my 27-year-old brother. My siblings and I also lost our parents as the death of my brother emotionally triggered an early onset of Alzheimer's in my mother, and my father gave the last four years of his life to a desperate search for my brother's body and those who had murdered him."[7] Bishop Carcaño is a gun violence trauma survivor who is speaking out.

Another mother, Sue Klebold, found her way through her pain by writing. She lost her son Dylan in what she refers to as a murder/suicide. One terrible morning her son armed himself and along with a peer gunned down students and teachers inside his Columbine high school in Colorado. To offer apologies for all that

> Sometimes the best recovery plan involves turning pain into protest and prevention.

she didn't know and to reach out to other parents, she wrote a best-selling book, *A Mother's Reckoning: Living in the Aftermath of Tragedy*.[8] Parents and family members may need to write, teach, advocate, lobby, and use social media to call attention to the need to protect other families from gun violence. Sometimes the best recovery plan involves turning pain into protest and prevention.

In an essay about the aftermath of gun violence, Gregory Gibson, who lost his sister to gun violence in the form of suicide and his son to a school shooting, described what his loss was like.

> When you suffer a loss like this, it feels like this: Not only has my loved one died, I have died as well. My former life, the life I would have lived with that now-dead loved one, exists no more. . . . Because we don't know we're grieving for ourselves as well as our loved ones, we can't get to the source of our grief, and it comes to seem bottomless, as if the world were made of grief. But somehow we survive. It's amazing how many of us survive.[9]

Lamentation for lost children is so deeply felt that survival is truly remarkable. Parents whose children are kidnapped at gunpoint have an even more complicated grief process. A kidnapped child's parents live without closure in the space between life and death. These parents feel guilty moving forward and regularly have to look backward. They live in a purgatory that continues without resolution.

Gun Violence in African American Communities

From one generation to the next, black experience in America includes extreme violence that inflicts multiple traumatic wounds.

> A kidnapped child's parents live without closure in the space between life and death.

Data from the Centers for Disease Control and Prevention show that of the 12,979 firearm homicides in 205, 81 percent occurred in urban areas. CDC data also show that within our nation's cities, black Americans are, on average, eight times more likely to be killed by firearms than those who are white. The rate of death by gun homicide for black people exceeds those among whites in all fifty states.[10]

False assumptions about black victimization abound, including those touted by politicians who reinforce myths that all blacks live in urban areas plagued by drug deals and gangs. Statistics show that blacks living in white neighborhoods have a greater chance of being shot than those in urban areas. Systemic racism and economic ceilings leave people of color in urban areas facing daily gun violence. According to Everytown for Gun Safety Support Fund, an organization dedicated to understanding and reducing gun violence in America, "Black men are 13 times more likely than white men to be shot and killed with guns." They are only 14 percent of the population but are the victims of one half of all gun homicides.[11] These deaths are often at the hands of white shooters. Mass shootings are overwhelmingly the actions of white men. The black community wisely points out the need for America to pay closer attention to the rage and gun violence among young white males.

Centuries-old white privilege, the tyranny of capture and slavery, white identification with the chosen ones of Israel, and professing Christians promoting the doctrine of Manifest Destiny have all contributed to the ongoing violence against black bodies. Spreading the idea that black bodies are inferior, proponents have ignored their suffering bodies and left them on the lynching tree or lying in the street. Then adherents to the dominant white ethos can turn their shame into blame, saying "They brought it on themselves." This doubly victimizes black families and ignores black parents' losses and their trauma. The parents experience double the trauma, first by death and then by oppression's diminishment. The police officers' disregard for Michael Brown's human dignity—they left his body in the street uncovered as neighbors and family stood helplessly by for hours—was so heinous I cannot find words for it. I believe that God lay in the street with Michael Brown in Ferguson, Missouri, on the day he was shot and during that long ordeal. God is still weeping there.[12]

The Black Lives Matter movement emerged in response to recurring trauma, cofounded by Alicia Garza, Patrisse Cullors, and Opal Tometi, three women with a passion for social justice. Black theologian John Richards notes that due to repeated brutality

> The black community wisely points out the need for America to pay closer attention to the rage and gun violence among young white males.

against them, African Americans have "held on to God's sovereignty, despite our trials."[13] Richards also points out the vital role of collective lamentation in healing the black community.

Domestic Violence and Gun Violence

As testimony began in the federal prosecution of Noor Salman, the wife of Omar Mateen, who killed forty-nine people at the Pulse nightclub in Orlando, Florida, in 2016, the connection between gun violence and domestic violence came into public awareness. Should she be held accountable for participation in his crime, if she was acting in fear for her own life following his intimidating control over her? She reported that her husband repeatedly abused her physically and emotionally. He punched her, choked her, threatened to kill her, coerced her into sex, and isolated her—all common tactics used by perpetrators in intimate partner violence.

According to law professor Deborah Epstein and domestic violence advocate Kit Gruelle, there is a demonstrated link between intimate partner violence and mass shootings. Many mass shooters have a history of violence in their families toward partners or children. Their intimidation tactics at home are similar to those used in their killing sprees. Devin Patrick Kelly entered a church and killed twenty-six people in Sutherland Springs, Texas. The Air Force had previously issued him a court-martial for domestic violence.[14]

Male rage, expressed at home and in mass shootings, cannot be minimized. Many families live in hiding and fear due to threats, intimidation, and retaliation. Women are taught in the culture and at church to sacrifice their own safety to save their husbands' souls. At church they learn to follow Jesus's path to the cross, reinforcing their sacrificial love to godly heights. A new theology is needed to assist abused women to claim the right to justice and protest against unyielding power. Jesus's path to the cross was not voluntary submission; it was outspoken protest against oppression and class dominance.

> Many mass shooters have a history of violence in their families toward partners or children.

Theologian Rebecca Ann Parker proclaims in her coauthored book with Rita Nakashima Brock, *Proverbs of Ashes: Violence, Redemptive Suffering, and the Search for What Saves Us*, that Christian theologians have too long reinforced abusive power and justified oppression. She writes,

> Theology that defines virtue as obedience to God suppresses the virtue of revolt. A woman being battered by her husband will be counseled to be obedient, as Jesus was to God. . . . A God who punishes disobedience will teach us to obey and endure when it would [instead] be holy to protest and righteous to refuse to cooperate.[15]

As Parker's words suggest, we need to entirely rethink the theological assertions that reinforce intimate partner violence.

When newlyweds Marti and John moved from a small college in Pennsylvania to a Boston suburb, they filled their pickup truck to the brim with household goods, book boxes, and hope. Friends had introduced them to each other in college and they dated for nearly a year before attending their June graduation ceremonies. A few weeks later they were married by the campus minister at a nearby Presbyterian church. John happily told everyone about his job offer at a big marketing firm in the city and Marti was looking forward to checking out graduate programs.

Marti thought she had seen John "at his worst," when he nearly had a nervous breakdown before finals at school. But after they settled into their Boston apartment the relationship began to crumble. John came home from his new job feeling stressed out and angry. He hated his new boss, who he said was "totally incompetent." He raged at Marti about his parents not paying more for his college tuition, so they could avoid mounting debt. Marti tried to be empathetic and to soothe him when he became red-faced and enraged. Nothing worked, and he began to turn his rage toward her. The dinner wasn't cooked right, the household not clean "enough" when he came home. He resented her daily freedoms and his new role as breadwinner. A few times he

> We need to entirely rethink the theological assertions that reinforce intimate partner violence.

let fly the "f" word regarding her laziness and how "easy" she had it. She was told to affirm him more, to have sex more often, to "make yourself look better," when he had work engagements she attended. His verbal battery shamed her, and she became frightened. She called her mother to find reassurance that this was the right marriage for her, but never told her about the escalating rage and verbal battery. Her mother encouraged her to find a job to help with the finances, but when she did John became even angrier. "I didn't want you to have to work," he said.

One night when he didn't get home as usual, she called him. In the background she could hear a bar or party. "Hey, what's up?" she asked. "Don't be calling me like this, it's embarrassing," he said, and hung up the phone. Later that evening, he staggered through the front door in a drunken rage. When she refused sex with him, he pulled a gun from the bedside table and held it to her head. She went totally limp in his arms and ceased her struggle, as he raped her.

Statistics indicate that guns are used to threaten and intimidate intimate partners in 69 percent of violent incidents. *The Journal of Women's Health* concludes a study on gun use in intimate partner violence, saying, "Weapon use of any type by an intimate partner is associated with a wide range of violent offender behavior and multiple negative outcomes for victims. The use of a gun has implications that include, but go beyond, physical injury of the victim."[16]

In 1994 the federal government passed a law called the Violence Against Women Act, which was amended in 1996. It prohibits people who have domestic violence restraining orders and those

> Statistics indicate that guns are used to threaten and intimidate intimate partners in 69 percent of violent incidents.

> As public outcry against gun violence rises, more states will join the movement to limit known batterers' rights to own guns.

Guns figure prominently in the violent lives and deaths of women. An estimated 4.5 million US women alive today have, at one time, been threatened with a gun held by their intimate partner. About 900,000 have been shot or shot at by an intimate partner. And when it comes to fatalities, women in the United States are more than twice as likely to be shot and killed by their male intimate as they are to be fatally shot, stabbed, bludgeoned, strangled, or killed in any other way by a stranger.[17]

with prior domestic violence misdemeanors from buying or owning firearms. Some (but not all) states have laws restricting batterers from purchasing guns. As public outcry against gun violence rises, more states will join the movement to limit known batterers' rights to own guns. Enforcement remains lax, and implementation remains challenging.

Marti had help from family and friends to end her relationship, which not all victims have. She had learned in college that domestic violence escalates and that it was not her fault. She believed in God's liberation for her life. She had the financial resources to get out and left when he was at work, leaving no forwarding address.

Victims typically hear many repentant speeches from their batterers. Many stay "for the sake of the children." Women who have trauma histories may have already decided that they are damaged goods and believe their partners' statements that they will never amount to anything or find love elsewhere. Some trauma survivors believe that they are strong enough to endure whatever befalls them, and so they stay in unhealthy relationships despite the abuse they receive. Male survivors of intimate partner violence feel doubly ashamed about abandoning their abusers. They are supposed to be manly enough to take it and to be in charge in such a way that no one batters them. Regardless of the gender or sexual orientation of the batterer, the escalation worsens when guns play a role in intimidation, assault, and death. More people than not have had their lives changed by a moment when a gun went off.

> More people than not have had their lives changed by a moment when a gun went off.

Emily's Story

At age sixteen, Emily fell in love with a fellow student in her Madison, Wisconsin, high-school youth group. They sang in a praise band and went on mission trips together. He was kind, handsome, and bright. She had an easy laugh that drew him toward her. They were a couple as sweet as any you'd meet. They talked of life together in marriage. And like other teens they pushed the boundaries to see what freedom feels like.

It was an unusual night when after going to the movies they went over to a friend's house. There were several teen boys there and no adults. Emily, who had a curfew, asked her boyfriend to drive her home by midnight, which he did. Her parents heard her come through the door and went off to sleep.

Her boyfriend went back to the friend's house and had a few more drinks with his buddies. He texted Emily now and then, expressing some fear, perhaps trying to stick it out due to peer pressure. And when he stopped texting, she sent a goodnight note and went to sleep. Next morning, at church, Emily was surprised he wasn't there. He was supposed to play music with her. And just as the pastor said the blessing, her phone rang and she heard the worst possible news.

Her nervous system was flooded with fear in those first few minutes; she doesn't remember the details. "I remember muffled sounds, the world turning from colors to grays, feeling like a zombie. I went to the restroom, and when people found me I wonder what I looked like. I just kept saying, 'He got shot, he got shot.'" She doesn't remember who helped her leave that restroom or what happened next. "It's as if I became two different people, one of them *not me*."

As Emily grasped for something solid at that moment, very little could provide her with grounding. Her body was awash in fear. Deep inside her brain, the mechanism that ensures survival clicked on, discarding unnecessary data and experiences. This is why it felt to her like she split apart that day. She was violently detached from her boyfriend and suddenly detached from everyone else—including herself.

Nine years later, while writing this book, I called Emily, and we talked about her trauma wound and her significant loss. Emily still doesn't know what happened to her boyfriend, and says, "That's the hard part, that it was so unclear!" Searching for details, she says, only made her trauma worse. She would sometimes conjure up frightening images of her boyfriend as he was dying. The shooter lied to neighbors and probably in court, so she wasn't going to contact him. And eventually she decided for herself (quite remarkably) that she would choose to "see" her boyfriend's last

> Tragically, more people are killed by the guns they keep in their homes than by strangers who enter those same homes. Children and teenagers can't tell how much danger they are in, especially when their judgment is impaired by alcohol. They don't know enough to be afraid. Fear is an emotion that develops over time by experiences with danger.

moments with little pain. She replaced her fearful imaginings with memories of a good day—a sunny day, walking together at the lake. She chose to remember them laughing together.

A neuroscientist would say that she rewired her brain to broaden neuropathways to include calm, security, and hope. Emily intuitively knew when it was time to stop asking the "why" questions that stay with victims until their pain eases up. "I will never know everything," she says. "I've accepted that knowing isn't going to change anything. . . . I want to remember the amazing person he was instead."

I asked Emily what helped her get through those first days and weeks. Her family stood by and offered help, even as they too grieved. Her boyfriend's family helped a lot too, especially his mother, who felt his loss most deeply. "I hung out, helping his mom heal. I also had people around me who didn't judge me. They told me there's no handbook for handling this, and they extended support." She found it hard to talk about, especially when she had to go back to school. "I cried through all my classes—in an ordinary lecture in English class—I cried and cried, and I didn't care." By not ignoring her pain or putting on a show for others, she stayed true to her own process.

Emily felt the loss as physical pain. She described her symptoms as chest pain, like maybe her "broken heart" had literally broken. She mourned her future in a loving partnership with a man who was her best friend and "soulmate." He appeared to her in dreams, and then she would have to awaken to the reality again. Those dreams were not comforting. Nothing was at first.

> Fear is an emotion that develops over time by experiences with danger.

But Emily instinctively knew how to heal herself. She wrote in a journal "without judging myself" and let the emotions have freedom to flow. After weeks in shock and despair when she went through the motions at school and retreated inside her safe spaces at home, she began to laugh a little bit now and then. She had a few objects that he'd given her and kept them close by. She let a family friend be her bridge back to her faith again.

Emily has become a young woman. She graduated from high school and met a man at college who created new possibilities for her, helped to heal her heart, and led her back to love. She now has a graduate degree in social work and works with at-risk children in an urban school.

She occasionally still dreams about her boyfriend. She looks at his Facebook page now and then and calls his cell phone. It took a few years before she could look at his texts from his last night. And when I asked her how it was to talk with me about her trauma, she slowed down a minute and said, "I feel tender, it feels like chest heaviness—it's sadness I can feel in my body." Her body holds memories.

Emily knows she had many advantages that other children and youth don't have after traumatic wounds. She had an extended network of support and many people she could call. She also told me what didn't help. She was particularly bothered when someone said, "God doesn't give you more than you can handle." For a while she was sure *it was too much*. She also knew that God wouldn't have taken away her future and her boyfriend's life one night with carelessness and a bullet. When people told her she was strong, it also rubbed her the wrong way. "Don't tell me I'm strong. I wouldn't choose to be strong . . . I did not feel strong." She insists that she did not heal by being strong either. "You just put one foot in front of the other, and you just go on living."

Emily's traumatic wound reshaped her life. Without having to have all the answers and with only a few formal sessions with a counselor,

> Loved ones who stood by her, saying "I will be here for you" and "You are safe with me," even before she could reach back, made all the difference.

Emily is currently healing and already healed. She listens deeply to and affirms her own process. Throughout her journey through grief, she stayed thankful for the love of her family and friends. Loved ones who stood by her, saying "I will be here for you" and "You are safe with me," even before she could reach back, made all the difference. And now she makes that difference for other victim/survivors.

A Final Note

Recovery, they say, takes a whole community. Prevention will take a whole nation, people of faith demanding an end to killing and proclaiming a theology that affirms resistance rather than sacrifice. As more and more victims shout not only in anguish, but also in protest, we can build a hopeful future.

For Reflection and Discussion

1 In the Hebrew Scriptures, Rachel's weeping is both literal and symbolic. Where do you find inconsolable grief in current events?

2 What facts about gun violence in this chapter surprised you most?

3 If you feel safe talking about it, describe gun violence you or a loved one experienced and what changed thereafter.

4 What action steps can you or your faith community take in response to gun violence?

Part Three
Pathways to Hope and Healing

8
Becoming Spiritually Whole Again

MELISSA WAS rushed to the emergency room seven months into her pregnancy due to severe bleeding. Expecting to have a healthy, full-term baby, she was told by the nurse in the delivery room that the doctor could not detect a heartbeat. The baby had inexplicably died in utero. Hours later when they laid her silent, beautiful son on her chest she cried uncontrollably, repeating these words: "Why, God, why did you do this to me?" Her lamentation chilled the room.

When trauma takes place, whether just this week or years ago, whether it was the loss of a baby, injury from gun violence, sexual abuse, natural disaster, or a tragic accident, every survivor asks "Why?" Why did the Boston Marathon bomber place that bomb in the trashcan near my family? Why did the hotel security guard ignore the huge black bags that the shooter carried to his room, bags full of weapons and ammunition he would use to gun down my friend at a country music festival? Why did that young man start shooting us during our Bible study class? Why was my child killed by a stray bullet? And survivors who saw people die in their living rooms, a coliseum, a church sanctuary, a synagogue, a nightclub, or a movie theater also ask, "Why? Why was I spared?"

Becoming well again begins with "why" questions and the search for answers. Trauma takes a destructive toll on well-honed belief systems. I remember a psychology professor telling his class, "We couldn't get out of bed every day without a belief in our own safety." Call it a cognitive belief system or call it denial, believing we'll be fine keeps us from crumbling under mortality's weighty reality.

Why God?

"Why didn't God save my baby?" Melissa asked her grief group in the weeks following her loss. Like many trauma survivors, Melissa found that all of her relationships were shifting after her loss—including her relationship to God. Her husband and friends hovered around her not knowing what to say. They wanted to help and support her but felt uncertain how to connect. She felt like "a zombie," and she was "dazed" and "immobilized." And worst of all, she felt that she had been betrayed by the God she'd believed in as far back as she could remember. God shifted from being a safe-haven to being a cruel assassin.

Trauma upends faith. Everything survivors once trusted and believed shreds apart when unthinkable tragedies happen. Like many other survivors Melissa was angry that she felt utterly alone and abandoned. Most survivors' search for healing includes tough questions, some of which are directed at God. For example: "Why weren't you here for me when I needed you?" "Why did you let this happen?" "Are you all powerful or not?" "How can I turn to you, God, if I can no longer trust you?"

If you have lived through one or more traumatic experiences, you may struggle with philosophies and religious ideas that previously made sense to you—and then suddenly didn't. You may find it hard to hold on to a lifelong faith. Having felt quite unprotected and abandoned by God, you may direct your anger at God and turn away.

Some survivors turn toward God and cling to Jesus as they never have before. You may find entirely new ways to look at God and relate to God. You may want to explore or choose an entirely new spiritual path. If the tenets of a long-held faith tradition no longer

> Call it a cognitive belief system or call it denial, believing we'll be fine keeps us from crumbling under mortality's weighty reality.

> Trauma upends faith.

make sense to you, your healing process will include a search for new beliefs and spiritual rituals that foster healing.

A trauma wound is a call to reexamine personal identity and faith identification. Even people who say they had a very close relationship with God prior to trauma often feel that during and after their terror and loss, God disappeared altogether. Empathetic family members, friends, and colleagues cannot fully understand what the survivor has gone through, and it feels as if God can't either. One survivor who had this isolating experience was puzzled about why her faith wasn't any help at all in the beginning. She said, "It took a while for me to know God was crying with me."

> A trauma wound is a call to reexamine personal identity and faith identification.

Why Me?

Olivia grappled with traumatic stress symptoms after a devastating divorce, including sleep dysregulation, social withdrawal, excessive crying, and occasional suicidal thoughts. The day she learned that she couldn't keep her house in the financial settlement with her ex, she fell to the floor and sobbed. This ripping apart felt like death. And when she had quiet moments alone, all she could seem to focus on was the question, "Why me?"

"Why did this happen to me?" she asked her pastor Sylvia. "I did everything right. I stayed in the marriage despite an affair he confessed to. I worked hard to make sure he had good food, a pleasant home, and free time with friends. I supported his work. I was Martha Stewart in the kitchen, and playful in the bedroom. Why did he leave me?"

Her pastor, Sylvia, let Olivia's lamentation take its course.

"How do you answer your own 'why' question?"

"I don't," she said with anger. "It makes no sense to me. Everything I was taught about how to be a good Christian wife just didn't matter. Some years ago, when I told my mother about Ernie's affair, she said I should just forgive him and be more Christlike. She said my marital

> Faith communities and church friends can be particularly unhelpful in this stage of recovery. They may direct you to old platitudes or even suggest that your personal tragedy was part of God's plan. They may tell you that suffering will bring about good, and good can emerge on down the road; your suffering is not a sadist's divine plan. Ignore them. You have the right to take your time in figuring it all out.

problem was my cross of suffering, and my job was basically to fix it by self-sacrifice. Be nicer. Dote over him. Meet his every need. You know, things every woman is taught. And then you'll get to heaven, right? Meanwhile, it was hell."

Pastor Sylvia knew better than to offer old platitudes and easy answers. She considered Olivia's questions and respected them. Olivia was in the process of reclaiming her worth and it would take her a while to recognize that the pain in spurned love didn't mean that she was an unloving person, and that her ex-husband's long list of judgments about her weren't true. Olivia had done everything right according to her Christian upbringing, and she didn't reap any rewards for this. She'd been given a lousy deal and didn't want any part of her former belief system. Olivia was reshaping everything she had come to know about herself and Christian teachings. And she needed time for anger.

"I can't come to church anymore," she told Sylvia.

"Because?"

"Because I feel abandoned by God and my church."

"We didn't help you to hold your husband accountable in the marriage, did we?"

"Exactly. He gets off scot free. A friend told me that his coworkers actually congratulated him for having a young blonde at his side at the last convention. Like he gets a new prize, and I get to live in a small apartment with our kids and struggle to pay bills while I search for a better job. How fair is that?"

"Olivia," Sylvia gently said, "It's not fair, and I don't understand it either, but I think it'll become clearer for you later on. If I tried to answer these questions for you, they would be *my* answers, not yours. You'll be best off finding your own answers as you go through this transition. You can come and talk with me at any time. I will listen to your questions, witness your tears, and I will pray for you as you try to make sense of things."

When people are wounded by trauma, asking "Why me?" is both a quest for understanding and a call for justice. Olivia was on a quest. Sylvia knew to support her without giving her simplistic theological language or packaging. Sylvia's openness to going on the journey with Olivia is exactly what victims need from pastors, friends, and family as they try to make sense out of what happened to them. Building self-esteem takes a while during the healing journey.

Why Evil?

When trauma wounds, we ask, "Why is there evil in the world?" When I arrived in Petaluma, California, to serve as senior pastor at First United Methodist church, it seemed as if the whole town was asking this question. It had not been long since a beautiful twelve-year-old girl named Polly Klaas was kidnapped at knifepoint from her own bedroom during a slumber party. Her friends were in the room with her, and her mother was sleeping in the room next door. While authorities searched for her, even people who did not know her were struggling to understand this heinous evil and to explain it.

People who were uncomfortable with the question of evil in the world tended to offer simple platitudes. "God knows that something good will come of this," and "Everything happens for a reason." Simplistic answers failed to satisfy us when nine weeks later Polly was found dead. How could God have let this happen? Psychologist Robert Grant writes, "Only those who truly care and believe will demand that God explain him/herself. If loss and suffering are not questioned then they lose their power to transform."[1] As victims become survivors, their demands for explanation lead them not to easy answers but to a life rebuilt.

I faced my own formulaic and naïve ideas about evil when Polly Klaas died. As lead theologian in our church, it was my job to make sense of this horror through the tenets of our faith. I felt ill prepared and ill equipped. My theological upbringing and my three-year seminary education weren't up to the interpretive challenge. I was raised in progressive Christian circles where preachers rarely talked about individual or collective evil. They vaguely spoke about "sin" and said that it was erased by the love of Jesus on the cross. They didn't talk about Satan, and they didn't finger point when people strayed from the biblical way. They professed that all people are created in God's good image. These perspectives had guided my preaching for years, and I had been able to skirt around many hard questions.

I was raising a daughter who was Polly's age at the time of Polly's disappearance, and like Polly's mother, I too had been the parent asleep in my own room during a slumber party. The world of online friendships with strangers was only beginning to be seen as dangerous. And then, a man who had met Polly online took her from her bedroom while her friends watched helplessly. I personally and publicly had to admit it—there are people in the world who are intrinsically evil and do not, or *should not*, receive redemption.

As a psychologist, I assume that the murderer was a psychopathic individual who may have been trauma-wounded too. But I have questions. Why are some people born without compassion or the ability to weigh consequences before taking action? Can we blame brain dysfunction or genetics? Will neuroscience eventually crack the code of evil? I hope so. *Meanwhile, I staunchly refuse to justify evil by saying that good comes out of it.* Good may or may not come from evil. In the words of trauma survivor Rebecca Parker,

> As victims become survivors, their demands for explanation lead them not to easy answers but to a life rebuilt.

> We cannot comfort ourselves by saying God is testing us or offering us a blessing that we don't yet understand. We have to face the pain without this divine sanction. We have to learn to grieve full out and face forward, without covering over the realities of human cruelty and violence.[2]

As a theologian with a trauma viewpoint, I still have more questions than answers about where God is when tragedy strikes. These are questions only trauma victims can answer. Where was God when you were molested? Where was God when you were gunned down as bullets ripped through the Pulse nightclub? But I have learned to let the process unfold for survivors and to listen as they teach us all.

The "Why?" That Calls for Justice

On the way to healing, trauma survivors have personal recovery work to do resolving intense emotions, including anger. A wise teacher once told me that anger is a demand for love. It is also a passion for justice. If you are a survivor, please know that you have a right to go fully into your pain and anger. Anger is the expression of your pain. Don't let anyone else try to minimize your anger or talk you out of it. Over time it will dissipate and you will learn to set it aside and have greater control over it. But early in the process be patient.

Perhaps a passage from Psalm 139 will surprise you. In verses one through eighteen in the psalm, the author talks about God's watching over us throughout our lives. And then verse nineteen takes a radically different tone.

Today the Polly Klaas Foundation (www.pollyklaas.org) offers resources for the families of missing children. They have found nearly ten thousand missing children and helped to comfort and connect parents whose children are never found.

> O that you would kill the wicked, O God,
>   And that the bloodthirsty would depart from me—
> Those who speak of you maliciously,
>   And lift themselves up against you for evil!
> Do I not hate those who hate you, O Lord?
>   And do I not loathe those who rise up against you?
> I hate them with perfect hatred;
>   I count them as my enemies. (Ps 139:19–22)

Were these verses written by a trauma survivor? They could have been. When death comes close to home, or human cruelty leads to abuse, the psalm writer asks God—who typically commands us to love our enemies—for permission to fully hate evil and wickedness. I give you permission to feel and acknowledge hate.

Trauma wounds call us to examine our emotional shadows where strong feelings live, to heal them, and to take them out into the world to claim and proclaim justice. After Consuela learned about her sister's gang rape at college, she felt such powerlessness and disgust that she vomited uncontrollably for months. She turned her pain inward, and depression overcame her—until the day she reached down far enough into her emotional chaos to find her anger. That day she began to sit up straighter, use her strong voice again, scream out, and hate her sister's abusers "with perfect hate." Her name itself means "consolation," and yet her healing required her firm refusal to be consoled. Her strong feelings both surprised and motivated her. She is still seeking justice by working to change campus cultures that minimize sexual violence.

A father received a knock on his door. When he opened it and saw two servicemen in dress uniforms, he knew instantly that his son had been killed in combat. For months he masked his sadness by letting the heroic emotion, anger, take over.

"I was raised that the Bible says not to be angry. I was told that being angry was a sin," he told the chaplain. "But who should I be angry at? Myself for supporting my son's decision to join the army? My wife

> Trauma wounds call us to examine our emotional shadows where strong feelings live, to heal them, and to take them out into the world to claim and proclaim justice.

when she cries and it hurts me so deeply to see her like that? God for not sparing him?"

"If we took out the 'should' part of that, who *are* you angry at?" the chaplain asked.

Choking back tears, he finally released his anger. "Everybody!" he said.

Trauma victims need anger's powerful energy as they move emotionally from being victims to being survivors. The students at Marjory Stoneman Douglas High School in Parkland, Florida, took their terror and transformed it into anger. They shouted out into their community and drew national attention to their cause, joining other gun-violence victims from mass shootings at schools across the country. Calls for justice have healed lives and changed our communities. Protestors marched to Selma, Alabama, took over cities like Ferguson, Missouri, and Sacramento, California, after young black men were shot in the back. Act Up marches advocated for LGBTQ civil rights and paved the way to get funding that developed better AIDS treatments. Women holding candles at Take Back the Night rallies brought public awareness to the injustices faced by rape victims. These actions moved people from disempowerment to strength.

Anger is one of the most basic emotional tools in the human psyche. When we tap into our anger, levels of testosterone rise, and a complex biological process prepares us for battle. We can feel powerfully alive and raise our voice and call for justice. Anger sets the cardiovascular system into motion, prompting sweating, releasing adrenaline, and preparing the body for action. The body is designed this way—to give us the strength to move from fear to action. The feeling of anger, at low decibels on the emotional Richter scale, is very useful.

But, I need to add a word of caution. When anger rises in the physical body and leads us to act in rage or violence, it is exceedingly dangerous. Too much constant anger leads to strokes,

> Trauma victims need anger's powerful energy as they move emotionally from being victims to being survivors.

> Some of the world's most famous pacifists have been very angry.

heart attacks, chronic stress syndromes, and loss of sleep, headaches, and many other physical symptoms.

If you are a trauma victim and your anger flares too often or too quickly, it's time to get help with it. If it leads to rage, swearing, physical abuse, threats, or property damage, it's a really huge problem, and you must address it. It will not help or heal your trauma at that level. Anger that flashes up quickly is not helpful to the body and destroys relational attachment. You can't listen to anyone if your pulse rate is up past 100 beats per minute; your hearing actually shuts down. You can't resolve a problem while adrenaline is coursing through your body. This type of anger is a symptom of lingering trauma and serves no positive purpose. At that point, your trauma anger could be more a call for vengeance than a call for justice. Until you have safely worked through your reactive emotions and life has become manageable, let others cry for justice and join the march for peace. Down the road in your healing journey, when you feel well enough and your emotions are back within your control, your voice and your witness are needed too.

> You can't resolve a problem while adrenaline is coursing through your body.

When "WHY?" Becomes "Why?"

As a trauma survivor you will likely always experience some remaining "why?" questions. Learning to take those questions with a lighter spirit can help the healing. They don't have to go away, but you can learn to live with them and set them aside. If, for example, you wrote a really big WHY on a piece of paper and held it up in front of your nose, all you could see is that word. You couldn't see a friend in front of you, the window across from you where the drapes are fluttering slightly, the mug on your coffee table. The word is all you see.

That's what it's like living with a large WHY. As you heal, turn over the paper and write it again in lowercase letters. Then move it away from your nose to the chair or floor near you. If you have to pick it up again, it's there for you. But now it's on the periphery in your life. It's true, you may never find all the answers (welcome to being fully human), but you can move on and experience positive emotions again. When you lay the paper aside you can see other words like *love*, *hope*, *healing*, *justice*, and *connection*. You can literally see the world around you where you are safe again, beauty exists, and people are nearby for support.

For Reflection and Discussion

1. Recall a time in your life when you felt utterly alone, or a time when God seemed to have abandoned you.

2. How did you become reconnected to God, or did you?

3. The psalmist writes, "I hate them with perfect hate" (Psalm 139). In what circumstances would it feel okay to have pure hatred, and what are the dangers in this feeling?

4. When has trauma called you to question or reshape your former beliefs?

9
Next Steps in Healing

Six months after her husband's funeral, Melissa asked me, "How do I begin to heal?" They had been together twenty years. As a local high-school football coach, Sonny was in good physical condition, and everyone was totally shocked when he died from a heart attack during practice. Melissa and Sonny had three young children. When she reached out for therapy, the initial shock and numbness was wearing off, and family members had returned to their homes and normal activities. The children, while often terribly sad, were supported by school staff and peers. But Melissa felt utterly alone, even when her children and friends were nearby.

We made a plan together to help her through the trauma. We assessed her symptoms and she made some initial behavioral changes. She became familiar with her emotional triggers so she could respond to them more quickly. I let her set her own goals for change, which gave her back a sense of control after a loss that was totally beyond her control. In all of these steps I affirmed her ability to move through and beyond trauma. She had a rough go at first, but she also had a resilient spirit, and it was a gift to witness her recovery.

IN THIS chapter I'll be talking about symptom awareness, secondary trauma, reaching out for help, the advantages of working with a trauma-informed therapist, and specific treatments. Whether you have directly experienced trauma as Melissa did or experienced it indirectly through loved ones, your church community, a friend, or community service, this chapter offers ways to reduce trauma's impact and foster resilience and healing.

> To prevent flu, you get an inoculation. Sometimes after the shot you still get the flu, but you are hit with milder symptoms. While trauma is wildly unpredictable, survivors and caring responders can build up their psychic "immune" systems. Clearing away old trauma wounds is a form of stress inoculation that can lead to milder and more manageable symptoms.

Paying Attention to Symptoms

The first task for trauma survivors after equilibrium returns is to pay attention to their emotions and physical symptoms. Melissa had to recognize that she couldn't get well again without getting more sleep. "I just hate to go to bed, because he's not there beside me," she said. But after six months of surviving on four to five hours of sleep per night, she was growing more depressed. She was also starting to "snap at the kids," which she didn't like but brushed off and minimized. Letting off steam was one of Melissa's coping patterns. She had grown up in a military home. "We don't have room for emotions," she said, "we just soldier on." In her situation this pain avoidance was making her worse instead of better. Her first healing step had to be to acknowledge and accept her own condition.

While working with Melissa I began to contemplate my own symptom avoidance. I had experienced secondary trauma over many years, but minimized trauma's lasting toll. Like other first responders, clergy, chaplains, and mental health professionals, I expected myself to handle many people's problems and witness their enormous suffering and remain unaffected.

There are cultural norms among clergy and lay servant leaders in churches that also lead to symptom denial, burnout, and exhaustion. I learned my propensity to minimize secondary trauma as a pastor. I recall an intense debate that arose at a conference in the United Methodist Church when clergywomen who were caring for children and elderly parents asked the voting body to approve less than full-time appointments for them. Conflict erupted on the assembly floor, and each microphone had a dozen people standing behind it waiting for a chance to talk. One pastor said, "Working anything less than eighty hours a week is a shame to Christ's calling." Another yelled simply, "There's no such thing as part-time ministry!"

The assumption that pastors must sacrifice themselves for others (after the example of Jesus) led Episcopal priest Barbara Brown Taylor into a vocational crisis, described in her book *Leaving Church*: "While I knew plenty of clergy willing to complain about high expectations and long hours, few of us spoke openly about the toxic effects of being identified as the holiest person in a congregation."[1] In too many vocational settings, "holy" professionals don't allow themselves to take time off for vacations or self-care—largely because they don't acknowledge their stress. They don't recognize their sleep loss, ruminating thoughts, hypervigilance, and addictive behaviors as symptoms of trauma.

Subtler trauma symptoms many professionals experience include lowered motivation, spiritual malaise, and emotional flatness while doing formerly pleasurable activities. A colleague with traumatic stress took less time off to be with his loved ones, stopped exercising, and lost his sense of humor. Secondary trauma may show up as mental rumination and hypervigilance. My colleague couldn't quiet his mind during yoga, brief meditations, and prayer, but he didn't recognize these problems as secondary traumatic stress. The psyche is masterful at denial and minimization.

I didn't own up to my own stress symptoms until one day when a doctor told me that an annoying physical problem was potentially life-threatening. The doctor suggested (of course) that stress was playing a major role in my condition. It was my body that got my attention.

How had I accumulated trauma? I had often walked alongside many loving and lovely people who became ill, suffered greatly, and died way too suddenly or at too young an age. After I became a psychologist, I worked like a first responder when tragedy struck. Wounded people brought their trauma to my office every day. As I held an emotionally safe space for my client's pain, I also

> Any therapist, pastor, or caring family member who has walked alongside a trauma survivor will also experience trauma.

> If you are reading this book to help others who have experienced trauma, I hope you will pay close attention to your own emotional and physical wellness. If you have heard the call of God in your life to serve among people at their moments of great need, you will need great courage and a few strategies to minimize trauma's transference in order to activate healing within yourself and be a healer for others.

experienced their powerlessness, their sadness, and their anger at the injustices they faced during and after trauma wounding. Any therapist, pastor, or caring family member who has walked alongside a trauma survivor will also experience trauma.

Not everyone who works with trauma survivors has the same level of resilience, the same personal support system, or the same faith practices. But a key factor in personal wellness for survivors and helpers alike is to pay attention to symptoms. Trauma symptoms kept a schoolteacher awake all night after ICE agents arrested the parents of several children in her classroom. Volunteers who travel across the country or beyond our borders to help restore hope after natural disasters often return home feeling overwhelming sadness and fatigue. Churches that adopt refugee families, provide shelters in fire-ravaged communities, and hold funerals for those whose lives were cut short by gun violence are both heroic and at risk. Yes, a whole church can become immobilized by secondary trauma! Because trauma is transferable.

Family Trauma Transference

When a rock is thrown into a pond, the impact is felt most strongly near the center where the rock entered the water. In a similar way, loved ones who are closest to trauma victims are at greatest risk for upheaval. Secondary trauma is common in the parents, spouses, and children of returning war veterans, among close-knit immigrant families, deportees' children, and the partners of rape victims. Trauma symptoms affect everyone who is holding a hand, standing at a bedside, passing a tissue, and watching with heartache for a dissociated loved one to return to joy and life again.

> Yes, a whole church can become immobilized by secondary trauma!

> While trauma victims tend to downplay the possibility that trauma has given rise to their symptoms, they may also be oblivious to secondary symptoms in others around them.

While trauma victims tend to downplay the possibility that trauma has given rise to their symptoms, they may also be oblivious to secondary symptoms in others around them.

I met with Stu every week for nearly a year before he finally felt safe enough to tell me about a turning point in his life. He and his girlfriend had been hitchhiking throughout the Southwest one winter when a car pulled over and picked them up. They sat in the front with the driver, who forced them to smoke joints and drink with him while he made jokes. Way out in the middle of the desert he pulled over to the side of the road and said it was time for "even more fun." He pulled out a knife and demanded that they walk down a path with him, where he told Stu's girlfriend to strip for him, and then, while he held a knife to her throat he raped her. Stu watched in stunned horror, while he begged the man to spare their lives. After the assault, the assailant got back into his car and drove away.

Stu suffered unending remorse and self-loathing because he had not protected his girlfriend. He had, over twenty-five subsequent years, written a dozen alternative endings to the story in which he'd gotten her free. In some of his scripts he'd killed the man before the rape was completed, in others he'd sacrificed himself as she fled for her life. But he could not escape his own memory. He was sleep-deprived, irritable, and depressed.

When Stu started coming to therapy nearly twenty years later, he was in a solid marriage of fifteen years and had a thirteen-year-old daughter at home. He'd recovered from years of alcohol abuse, which he had used to keep his trauma symptoms at bay. Then, without the alcohol to numb him, he started having panic attacks.

In therapy he found ways to focus on his strengths, to forgive himself for his powerlessness, and to resolve his pain about the girl. Even though he had no idea where she was living or how to find her, he wrote her a soul-wrenching apology. The panic attacks slowly dissipated and therapy seemed complete. We said goodbye and I closed the file.

When the phone rang about six weeks later and it was Stu, I was surprised. He called to tell me that his daughter had started having panic attacks—"Out of the blue!" he said. It was as if the family system had relied on someone being overly stressed all the time, and when Dad got well, the daughter took on the sickness. This is not uncommon. Children often bear emotional symptoms for their parents. In Stu's case a family therapist was called in to help them all release the emotional symptoms that Stu's trauma had brought into their lives.

It's not uncommon for clergy, lay servants, and therapists to take on emotional symptoms that are not rightfully theirs. A church is a family system. Early in my career as a pastor, a colleague told me that I just needed to "armor up" and "get thicker skin" in order to serve God's people. I resisted the idea that I had to get tougher and be less open-hearted. I learned instead to see my ability to enter into someone else's suffering as a good thing and then to balance it with lots of self-care practices, including spiritual direction. As the "parents" in the church family system, it is essential that clergy model health and wholeness rather than exhaustion and burnout.

Sometimes the hardest step is the first phone call. Whether a police officer is calling the Employee Assistance line, a college student is going to the campus counseling center following an assault, a flood victim is spending an hour with a psychologist after a hurricane, or a veteran is calling the domiciliary, the first call takes great courage. "It felt like admitting defeat," a veteran said. While PTSD classes were offered to returning vets in our community, those who attended were mocked by their peers as being unmanly and weak. Many trauma victims avoid that first call because they don't want to have to tell their story, or they fear that diving into the pain will make them feel worse instead of better. Some people delay that call for months, years, and decades. Research clearly shows that mental and emotional readiness to address trauma is a very individual process.

> Children often bear emotional symptoms for their parents.

> Sometimes the hardest step is the first phone call.

Crisis Interventions

Pastoral counselors, clergy, and laity who are called into service need to understand the limitations of their training in responding to trauma-wounded people and communities. I watched a news interview where a television anchor spoke with a man who had intervened in gun violence and taken down a shooter. It was just a day after the event. The "hero" (so named by the commentator) was clearly in shock. He listened carefully to the questions and took a while to respond. He seemed to be searching for his memories of what happened. He may have been understandably anxious about being on the national news, but I believe he was in post-traumatic shock. The scene was still so fresh that his brain didn't know how to organize his thoughts about it. He didn't consider himself to be a hero, and yet, here was a national newscaster calling him this. The man had witnessed a shooting death and had been grazed by gunfire and injured during his fight with an assailant. And he was absurdly expected to make sense of that just twenty-four hours later.

For decades, psychologists have come alongside trauma victims. They were there at 9-11 in New York City to assist first responders. They were in New Orleans after the floods from Hurricane Katrina. And researchers have now studied the traumatic incident debriefing techniques they used. What they learned after studying the outcomes for trauma survivors is that asking them to speak about terrifying details early in the process actually made it more likely that they would develop PTSD. Telling the story to a sympathetic listener before symptoms had calmed down, when adrenaline was still high, and undifferentiated emotions were overwhelming the right brain, seared the trauma into their memories in a deeper and longer-lasting way. This research altered treatment protocols following disasters. Rather than elicit the story of what happened, early interventions now focus on self-care, tools for getting good sleep, encouragement to engage with loved ones and to seek prescription medication if necessary while avoiding stress relievers such as alcohol and unhealthy eating. Telling the story comes much later in the healing process.

In the television newscast I watched, the anchor was asking the "hero" to tell a story he had no way to fully comprehend and by so doing may have impeded his recovery. In the initial days and weeks after trauma, people around victims need to let them decide when and if talking will help. Pastors, loved ones, lay servants, and counselors can create safe space for the story to be told eventually, but should not ask for it prematurely. At any time, referral to a trauma therapist is a good plan.

Trauma Informed Therapy

When I decided to clear out my accumulated secondary trauma, I called around to find someone who understood my symptoms. For a few months, I climbed a set of stairs to Nola's safe space. As I told her about many, many stories that contained horror, death, and sexual assault, she helped me to focus on the scenes I had not yet physically or mentally been able to release. Using a technique called Eye Movement Desensitization and Reprocessing (EMDR), Nola helped me to lower my psychoactive responses to my worst traumatic memories. We cleared away accumulated emotional fragments one after another. When I was finished with these treatments, I could still recall incidents when I chose to, but they had less physiological arousal connected to them. I felt tremendous relief. By six months later, my doctor was pleased to announce that my physical symptoms had entirely resolved.

How do you know if you have a trauma-informed therapist? Trauma-informed therapists take several specific approaches.[2]

> Eye Movement Desensitization and Reprocessing (EMDR) is a neurocognitive treatment approach, which is particularly useful for treating post-traumatic stress disorder (PTSD). The client holds buzzers in each hand or watches the therapist's fingers move from side to side while a traumatic memory is recalled. By using bilateral stimulation, scrambled memories cross over the hippocampus "bridge" from the right brain into the logical left brain, and anxiety is reduced. Recalling these memories during a calm state reduces their ongoing emotional and physical disturbance. Read more at EMDR: Eye Movement Desensitization and Reprocessing—WebMD, https://tinyurl.com/ycf54c3x.

They believe that it is important to establish a safe therapeutic environment where any topic can be addressed with compassion and acceptance. They monitor their responses to their clients' stories to be sure they aren't responding with avoidance, shame, or shock. Then, they view trauma-related symptoms as normal adaptations to traumatic experience. Withdrawal, panic, cutting, dissociation, and even conflictual relationships are viewed as strategies developed after trauma to keep life from completely falling apart. Trauma survivors are sometimes labeled "drama queens" or "control freaks," or they say these phrases about themselves. Without judgment, trauma-informed therapists view negative self-talk and shame responses as the clients' coping mechanisms, and then encourage survivors to replace negative self-talk with positive statements leading to beneficial change.

> Trauma-informed therapists believe that full recovery is achievable.

Lastly, trauma-informed therapists believe that full recovery is achievable, and while they directly address symptoms, they see trauma recovery as the primary treatment goal. While most trauma survivors go to therapy initially for anxiety or depression, it's essential to trace these symptoms back to their traumatic origins and then to treat both the trauma wound and any accompanying mental health symptoms. Trauma-informed therapists work collaboratively with victim/survivors to enhance strengths and avoid a focus on pathology.

Unfortunately, therapists can damage a survivor's self-esteem by labels and diagnostics. At the very first appointment, a therapist has to fully assess many complicated aspects of the client's wellness and dysfunction. On medical insurance forms, a diagnosis is usually required at the first session. Many clients begin to think of themselves as—fill in the blank with a diagnosis—instead of people adapting to harsh, painful, and stressful circumstances. I got a call from a woman one day looking for a therapist, and she said that she was bi-polar, borderline, currently depressed, and a trauma victim. I paused a moment and asked her to start her introduction over. "I'd like to know who *you* are when you strip away all those labels. You are more than your diagnoses or past experiences." This took her aback for a minute and then she said, "That sounds great, when I can come in?" This is an example of the way that a trauma-informed therapist works to personally affirm clients and make use of client resiliency.

Letting a survivor set the pace and the goals during recovery gives the client power and self-worth. Skills can be taught to reduce symptoms like flashbacks, dissociation, emotional dysregulation, high levels of anxiety, and distorted thinking. Yet the goals must be set by the survivors themselves.

Connie had been coming to see me for therapy once a week for many months when one day she asked me if she could bring her poetry to share. She had been repeatedly sexually abused by her swim coach when she was a teenager. I knew that part of her abuser's seduction had been to exchange poetry with Connie, and this could have been an unconscious attempt to reenact a boundary crossing or to test me a bit. I was glad that she trusted me enough to share her feelings with me in session and yet cautious. With a little more inquiry it became clear that Connie expressed herself through her journals and poetry—and even planned to publish her poetry as a way to help other victim/survivors. So I welcomed her bringing them to the next appointment.

She came in the next week and gave me an amazing poem describing with searing clarity her abuser's behavior and her horrifying experience. I read it, and then I handed it back to her. "This is incredible," I said. "I want you to keep it," she said. And this was the moment when I could help her take back her power. "Connie, I don't want to keep this in your file, because it belongs to you, not me. It's not mine to pass along, and I would have to do that if your file was called for review by an insurance company, or I was subpoenaed to present the file in a lawsuit. I won't do what your abuser did and take something this precious, private, and intimate away from you." Connie was silent as tears streamed down her face, and she released more of the pain she had felt for over thirty years.

Therapy with trauma victims must involve empowerment. Trauma-informed counselors take a one-down position in order to let their

> Letting a survivor set the pace and the goals during recovery gives the client power and self-worth.

> Self-efficacy is the power and ability to accomplish one's own goals. People with self-efficacy believe they can overcome obstacles. They may have been victimized, but the word *victim* doesn't define them.

clients lead the way. They are careful to never use their power to minimize the client's power or exert abusive control. Trauma renders one powerless in every way. Therapy, pastoral care, and helping volunteers need to be mindful that their job is to give victims back their power, esteem, and self-efficacy.

Suffering Alone Is Not Heroic

Reaching out to others can make the difference between getting stuck as a victim and moving toward the liberation that comes with being a survivor. Supportive community can make all the difference!

A war veteran didn't speak for two years after he watched his fellow soldiers die in a bomb blast in Iraq. He was so disconnected that he couldn't help his wife and children, who suffered intensely. A cousin in the family took the man in. She read to him every day. And he had only a blank expression on his face. She sang songs and played the piano. He said nothing. She encouraged him to sit out on the porch with her and watch the birds in the yard. She helped him to notice the first crocuses that came up in the springtime and the robin's return to her feeder. When the nights grew warm, they stood out in the yard together. She pointed out the North Star and let him know that he would find his way again, even though he was in darkness and pain. Without training and with great love, she gently held space for his suffering. Believing that he would return to life when he was ready, she became his North Star. And one day when she returned to the house with groceries, she found him digging weeds out in the garden, and when he shouted "hello," he smiled broadly. She nearly dropped the bag in disbelief and joy, knowing he was finally back.

Help can be found among people with great love and compassion who believe in recovery and each person's ability to experience resurrection. They become North Stars. And for those who seek recovery through pastoral care and therapy, trauma-trained helpers can hold space so that the darkness is dotted with points of light until the dawn returns.

For Reflection and Discussion

1. Recall a time in your life when your body warned you about your stress or trauma. Were you thankful for the message? Why or why not? What did you do next?

2. How does the culture at your church lead to burnout or promote self-care for clergy and lay volunteers?

3. When have diagnostic labels helped or hindered you or someone you love?

4. Who are the people in your life who have been North Stars?

10
Rediscovering Hope

IN THIS book you've been reading about the ways trauma devastates the body, the soul, and relational attachment. You've met trauma survivors who struggled with cognitive symptoms such as memory loss, dissociation, flashbacks, and nightmares. You've met survivors as they integrated feelings and thoughts after trauma wounding. And you've met survivors whose healing is taking a lifetime. You've met an eighty-year-old survivor who said, "Honey, you never get over it." You've met a young adult who overcame her first true love's death by gunfire and has become a counselor for teens. She is not finished healing, but her laughter, love, and faith have been restored.

If you are a trauma survivor, your healing journey can begin right now. A man came into my office in his mid-fifties to process his abuse as a teenager, a woman in her mid-seventies had physical symptoms that led her to a memory she wanted to work through and come to peace with. It's never too late to address the traumatic wounds in your own life. Healing can always begin *right now*.

In the next few pages, you will be reading about some therapeutic techniques that help survivors. A word of caution: the ideas offered here are not a form of psychotherapy or a substitute for trauma-informed therapy. If you are a survivor, please know that you are worth the time and cost involved in seeking help, building trust, and working through your wounds with the help of a therapist. Find a therapist who will let you work at your own pace and set your own goals. In therapy, you can draw upon your many innate healing capacities.

> If you are a trauma survivor, your healing journey can begin right now.

Each victim's recovery journey is as different as our thumbprints are from each other.

Jennifer's Healing Journey

Jennifer was sexually abused as a pre-teen by a babysitter who was also a distant cousin. She had little social support to help her through the trauma, no faith community, and no trusted teacher at school. Since her assailant was in her family and she was disbelieved by her parents, she lost all of her previously safe relationships at an early age. "I made a deal with myself," she said, "that I would protect myself at all costs—and the cost was isolation and loneliness." After a disastrous marriage and divorce, she began looking at the big picture to discover her part in the chaotic attachment patterns she had lived with. "I don't know how to build something more solid," she remarked. She had adapted to abuse by closing down her emotions and distrusting others, and she was about to embark on a terrifying quest to find herself again.

Jennifer's healing journey entailed claiming her pain when other people's words or actions hurt her and proclaiming her right to set healthy boundaries in her workplace and at home. I had her practice this key sentence over and over again with a calm firm voice, so that when she felt violated she could say, "That's not okay with me." When people around her tried to convince her that she was wrong about something she felt or believed, she brought out another sentence, "I can understand how you might feel that way," rather than capitulate to their ideas at the cost of her own integrity.

I introduced Jennifer to healthier lifestyle habits to support her mental health. Walking has been shown in multiple studies to increase serotonin and norepinephrine production, enhance endorphins, and reduce depression.[1] She started walking every other day for just twenty-five minutes, rain or shine. This reduced her depression, and so she slowly titrated off her antidepressant in about six months. She felt happier and less anxious after her walks and throughout the day.

We worked together to restore her sleep. Like many survivors, Jennifer hated bedtime and nighttime, because these were times when her brain would "run off into fear." Her abuse had taken place in the evenings and at her bedtime, so this was a deeply seated bodily memory too. The feeling of relaxation most people feel as they drift off to sleep was terrifying for Jennifer. She stayed up late watching television or scrolling around on her iPhone, which was making her sleep problem worse. Blue light screens can overstimulate the brain, reduce melatonin production, and in several other ways keep people awake.[2]

Jennifer resisted this behavior change more than many others. Being alone with her thoughts and feelings had always been daunting. Her mind not only raced around in old fear responses, her self-talk was often negative and self-critical. She had internalized the shame language others had doled out to her. I reminded Jennifer that she still had inside herself the positive and happy child she had been before the abuse. Imagining joyful feelings led her to claim them again. Imagining a kind child inside herself led her to kinder attitudes.

Jennifer eventually moved all electronics with blue-light screens out of her bedroom and listened to a CD she'd found with relaxing sounds and children's lullabies. She listened to the same music every night, just as her children had listened to a musical bear she wound up for them as they went to sleep. And when she awoke, she played it over again. This is a technique called "cued sleep" where the brain hears the music and sends sleep messages to the body. She also took her "inside kid" to the library and brought home children's books to read at night. This gave her a sense of joy and safety to replace the terror she'd been recalling for years.

"Sleep hygiene" is a term psychologists use to describe behaviors that can enhance a good night's sleep. Sleep hygiene can include reducing caffeine intake, setting and keeping a regular time for sleeping and waking, darkening the bedroom, avoiding blue-light screens for an hour before bed, avoiding sugary snacks at night, and leaving the "to do" list in another room before going to bed.

Jennifer learned to let her body relax throughout the day to enhance her sleep at night. She used a technique called progressive relaxation, which involves tightening and releasing the muscles throughout the body. By practicing this throughout the day, she actually taught herself to relax in any circumstance. When she was at work and couldn't do the whole exercise, she simply began the pattern by making fists and then relaxing her hands. The body knew how to take it from there, and every muscle relaxed.

I referred Jennifer to a yoga teacher who has a class specifically for trauma survivors. She learned a basic exercise—to pat herself when she was feeling stress. This simple patting technique (the way we pat babies) helps survivors regulate their nervous systems and reduce the fight, flight, and freeze response. During yoga the mind learns to focus on breathing and stretching, opposite actions for most trauma survivors who in great fear became and have remained knotted up in tension.

Much new research is being done on healing the neurobiology of trauma. The brain is a neuropathway for thoughts and emotions, and many new studies illustrate the way our brains shift during and after trauma. Luckily, our brains can also be trained to become calmer and less reactive, leading to feelings of peace and joy. Author and psychologist Rick Hanson has taken complex neurobiological concepts and made them accessible to everyday readers in his book *Hardwiring Happiness*.[3] Hanson asserts that the more we think happy thoughts, the more our brain opens pathways for increasing happiness.

Hanson's work builds upon theories by another trauma expert, psychologist Peter Levine, who became curious about the somatization of trauma. Somatization is simply the idea that our bodies hold trauma within them. Many of us have trauma we do not consciously recall until we thoroughly explore a pernicious physical symptom. Unresolved muscle pain may be a symptom that developed after a life-threatening fall, when we blocked an assault, or after having to stay alive by hiding for hours in a culvert to

> She used a technique called progressive relaxation, which involves tightening and releasing the muscles throughout the body.

> Many of us have trauma we do not consciously recall until we thoroughly explore a pernicious physical symptom.

avoid capture. Levine has spent his career researching the ways that trauma manifests in unconscious physical symptoms.[4] Many trauma survivors find that the very physical way they protected themselves could also be keeping them from healing. He believes that the key to living well again is to unlock these bodily secrets.

To build resilience after trauma, survivors need multiple ways to become acquainted with their physical symptoms and to calm and rebalance their bodies. In addition to yoga, Jennifer began using mindfulness meditations daily. She thought at first that all meditation practices were incompatible with her religion but found them to be similar to the practice of prayer. She chose a guided meditation app from among many she could get on her iPhone that best fit her busy schedule and seemed consistent with her value system and beliefs.[5]

Jennifer's work in recovery involved entire shifts in thinking. She stopped her habit of focusing on her ex-husband and began to focus instead on what she needed and wanted. She progressed through many stages that I call "claiming and proclaiming." She claimed her right to have and express many different feelings. She claimed her right to time for self-care, including fitness and meditation. Jennifer had never previously claimed her right to any happiness at all. But when she began claiming her abuse story and the shame fell away, she gained enough courage to proclaim to her remaining family members that their denial of her abuse had been and still was deeply painful. She examined her old tendency to withdraw and avoid, and proclaimed her power by turning toward others rather than away from them. As she engaged in this hard work, I watched Jennifer blossom into a fabulously solid new person.

If you are like Jennifer, please take hope from her story. Or if you have someone like Jennifer in your circle of friends and family, keep hope alive for their healing transformations. It has long bothered me that the church stops talking about Easter each spring after just one or two Sundays with peppy hymns, when every single day people all around us are singing resurrection songs.

Witnessing

Attending a public event for abuse survivors at a local temple, I could sense the audience honoring the sacred space in which stories were safely told. No one had been coerced to witness or attend. At events like these there are as many trauma stories that cannot yet be shared and many that will never be shared publicly. But painfully private stories are still healed by the witness of other trauma survivors.

Each trauma victim has a story to tell, and the story changes throughout the healing process. A story told too soon can increase symptoms of PTSD and delay neurocognitive healing. A coerced story is really a second type of trauma placed upon victims in, for example, "fear interviews" at centers for deportation, paperwork required by veterans to obtain disability checks, social workers' child protection interviews, and police interrogations. Workplace harassment complaints are typically written reports followed by intimidating interviews. Sometimes victims are forced to sit in rooms with their perpetrators during abuse resolution processes. These experiences are not healing; they retraumatize. Telling the story too soon, even to family members who aren't emotionally able to be supportive, can add another layer of fear and mistrust. Trauma survivors need time to carefully consider whom to tell, when to tell, what to tell, and the consequences that could follow. Being wounded and then disbelieved can be devastating.

But telling the story can also be liberating. It empowered students in Parkland, Florida, to turn toward cameras and let their lives become points of light in the movement to stop gun violence. Once a year, women in my community who have been raped go to the plaza for a nighttime rally, and holding lighted candles, they listen to each other's stories about victimization and redemption. Just think about the hundreds of organizations that have been launched by trauma survivors. We need these painful stories to be told so that we too can find our way when unthinkable tragedies happen. Trauma survivors' stories keep us mindful that, in the words of Barbara Brown Taylor,

> Every single day people all around us are singing resurrection songs.

> Each trauma victim has a story to tell, and the story changes throughout the healing process.

> We need these painful stories to be told so that we too can find our way when unthinkable tragedies happen.

"there is a light that shines in darkness which is only visible there."[6] And, in the first verses of John's Gospel, we find God's enduring promise that the darkness cannot and will not ever, ever, overcome the light (John 1:5).

Justice Seeking

I had a driveway moment last week. That's a moment when you sit in your car and finish listening to something compelling on the radio. I was singing along with one of Mavis Staples's resurrection songs. A client had acquainted me with her music when he gave me a CD he'd made containing songs that helped him recover from his trauma wounds. Her singable lyrics are infused with hope. Her melodies are rooted in songs written by people who were captured, separated from their land and their loved ones, sold and enslaved. They are rooted in the hope that endured despite torture, lynching, and sexual abuse. Amidst generational trauma, black Americans penned the musical themes that underlie American gospel, blues, and rap. In the song "No Time for Crying," Mavis Staples says sometimes we have to set aside tears, because "people are dying and bullets are flying," and we've all got work to do. It's a ballad that calls her listeners into justice work.

You've read many trauma survivors' stories in this book. I have been honored to know them. Facts about them have been changed in the book to protect their privacy, and I have created certain details within these stories. But I have stayed true to the experiences that are universal, while at the same time very private. I have shared my own trauma as well, both primary and secondary, with the goal that clergy and other mental health professionals reading this book will stay vigilant about their own self-care. Very few of us live a lifetime unscathed by the violence around us.

> Very few of us live a lifetime unscathed by the violence around us.

I have included war veterans in these stories, particularly their experiences returning home to their families. I have worked with women veterans who were sexually traumatized by fellow soldiers and by enemy combatants. Because I have limited experience working with combat veterans, I have not delved deeply into the many adverse mental health effects on them such as traumatic brain injuries, suicidality, domestic violence, and addictions that mask emotional symptoms. Nor have I explored the adverse outcomes most war veterans face in the military when their trauma symptoms are minimized and they are shamed for appearing to be weak when they reach out for help.[7]

I am strongly opposed to war, particularly knowing the breadth and depth of trauma wounding that wars create. I do not believe any war can justify death, the traumatic wounding of combatants and noncombatants alike, or mass migrations. In light of new research on multigenerational trauma, I believe that this devastation will lead to biological changes many children and grandchildren will inherit. I believe that when peace becomes more precious than gold, instead of waging battles, we will walk in Jesus's way and beat our swords into plowshares.

There are many other stories I haven't had room to include in the book. Human sex-trafficking victims who live in my community tell stories about their narrow escapes from pimps, and some of them are as young as fifteen. They have been repeatedly raped and had their lives threatened. They are speaking out now because they have a passion to get other women out of sexual slavery and they have created a safe house for recovery.

People in my congregation, and probably yours, have experienced medical trauma. They went to the hospital and were told the shocking news that they or someone they loved had only a few days left to say goodbye. Or they were traumatized over a false positive test for a cancer that never materialized. Today's modern medical system is both curative and trauma-wounding. There are too many traumatic experiences in any person's daily life for me to have covered them all.

Once you delve into the subject of trauma, you see it everywhere. Hearing the stories in this book, you likely found that you've had some traumatic experiences you hadn't previously recognized as

> As you've read along in the book, you have likely thought about additional types of trauma wounds in your life or among your family and friends. If you or someone you know is dealing with lingering or disturbing symptoms, you might explore a helpful workbook on healing called *P.T.S.D. Workbook: Simple, Effective Techniques for Overcoming Traumatic Stress Symptoms*.[8] A trauma-trained therapist can assist you or your loved one with this workbook.

such. After a workshop during which I presented a story about sexual harassment in the workplace, a woman approached me. She said something like this, "I had been telling myself a story—and that story was that my own harassment was a *small* thing. Now I know that it wasn't. It changed the trajectory of my career." That workshop gave her the awareness she needed to heal a powerfully traumatic wound from two decades earlier.

As people of faith, we are called to acknowledge and tenderly care for our own traumatic wounds. As we heal our lives, we help others to do the same. We are also called to create truly safe sanctuaries for refugees, gun violence victims and their families, returning veterans, and sexual abuse victims. We need to listen to trauma survivors' stories—especially the ones that make us uncomfortable. This is sacred work. When our sanctuaries shelter wounded souls, we help them to bear pain and hold out hope for their recovery.

For Reflection and Discussion

1. What have you learned from surviving trauma or from trauma survivors you have known? Describe someone whose trauma recovery story gives you hope.

2. Do you think it's possible to end war? If not, why not? If so, where would you start?

3. What scripture texts or songs do you lean on in troubled times?

4. What are your take-aways from reading this book?

Notes

Introduction

1. "It Is Well with My Soul," Wikipedia, https://tinyurl.com/ycwvo3b2.

Chapter 1: What Is Trauma?

1. Benedict Carey, "Holding Loved One's Hand Can Calm Jittery Neurons," *New York Times*, January 31, 2006.
2. This term is found in the writings of Eduardo Duran, *Healing the Soul Wound* (New York: Columbia University Press, 2006), 16.
3. "PTSD Statistics," PTSD United, https://tinyurl.com/qztfggh.
4. Bessel van der Kolk, Alexander McFarlane, and Lars Weisaeth, eds., *Traumatic Stress: The Effects of Overwhelming Experience on Mind, Body, and Society* (New York: Guilford, 1996).
5. "When Is It Trauma? Bessel van der Kolk Explains," *Psychotherapy Network*, January 11, 2017, https://tinyurl.com/y8yrml8x.
6. One in five women have been the victim of attempted or completed rape in their lifetime. Nearly one in two women have experienced sexual violence other than rape in their lifetime. One in five men have experienced a form of sexual violence other than rape in their lifetime. Twenty-seven percent of male victims of completed rape were first raped when they were ten years old or younger. Most female victims of completed rape experienced their first rape before the age of twenty-five and almost half experienced their first completed rape before age eighteen. See M. C. Black et al., *The National Intimate Partner and Sexual Violence Survey (NISVS): 2010 Summary Report* (Atlanta: National Center for Injury Prevention and Control, Centers for Disease Control and Prevention, 2011).

7. Black et al., *The National Intimate Partner and Sexual Violence Survey*, 161.
8. Van der Kolk et al., *Traumatic Stress*, 3.
9. Matthew J. Friedman, "PTSD History and Overview," US Department of Veterans Affairs, https://tinyurl.com/ybfxpolj.
10. Friedman, "PTSD History and Overview," https://tinyurl.com/ybfxpolj
11. "What Are Dissociative Disorders?" American Psychiatric Association, https://tinyurl.com/ybx32f5b.
12. See Russ Harris and Steven C. Hayes, *ACT Made Simple* (Oakland, CA: New Harbinger, 2009).
13. Charles Wesley, "And Are We Yet Alive," hymn 553 in *The United Methodist Hymnal* (Nashville: United Methodist Publishing House, 1989).
14. David Brooks, "Tales of the Super Survivors," *New York Times*, Nov. 24, 2015, https://tinyurl.com/y7m3kxm9.

Chapter 2: Trauma's Aftermath

1. Bessel van der Kolk, *The Body Keeps the Score: Brain, Mind, and Body in the Healing of Trauma* (New York: Penguin Books, 2014). While trauma literally rearranges the brain's wiring—specifically areas dedicated to memory, van der Kolk also describes ways to overcome this hardwiring.
2. Helen Fisher, "Your Brain in Love," TED Talk, https://tinyurl.com/gspp5hy.
3. American Psychiatric Association, *Diagnostic and Statistical Manual of Mental Disorders*, 5th ed. (Washington, DC: American Psychiatric Association, 2013), 271–73.
4. National Alliance on Mental Illness, https://www.nami.org/. Search for dissociative disorders.
5. Babette Rothschild, *The Body Remembers* (New York: W. W. Norton, 2000), 31.

Chapter 3: Disrupted Moods and Behaviors

1. Robert Grant, *The Way of the Wound: A Spirituality of Trauma and Transformation* (Oakland, CA: Self-published, 1996), 60.

2. A full examination of shame in Christianity and in faith communities can be explored in my previous books. Karen McClintock, *Sexual Shame: An Urgent Call to Healing* (Minneapolis: Fortress Press, 2001), and Karen McClintock, *Shame-Less Lives: Grace-Full Congregations* (Lanham, MD: Rowman & Littlefield, 2011).
3. Jules Woodson, "I Was Assaulted. He Was Applauded," Op-Ed page, *New York Times*, March 9, 2018, https://tinyurl.com/ycwta9j8.
4. William M. Kondrath, *Facing Feelings in Faith Communities* (Lanham, MD: Rowman & Littlefield, 2013), 2.

Chapter 4: Trauma's Damaged Relationships

1. Susan M. Johnson, *Emotionally Focused Couple Therapy with Trauma Survivors: Strengthening Attachment Bonds* (New York: Guilford, 2002), 3.
2. Mark Bekoff, "Grief in Animals: It's Arrogant to Think We're the Only Animals Who Mourn," *Psychology Today*, October 29, 2009, https://tinyurl.com/nvs5u2z.
3. Stephanie Watson, "Death of a Spouse or Partner Can Lead to Heart Attack or Stroke," Harvard Health Publishing, Harvard Medical School, February 27, 2014, https://tinyurl.com/ydh97g2j.
4. Johnson, *Emotionally Focused Couple Therapy*, 36.
5. Amir Levine and Rachel S. F. Heller, *Attached: The New Science of Adult Attachment and How It Can Help You Find and Keep Love* (New York: Penguin Group, 2011), 8–9.
6. Michael Fulwiler, "The Research: The Still Face Experiment," The Gottman Institute, March 25, 2013, https://tinyurl.com/ya3zrhfp.
7. Johnson, *Emotionally Focused Couple Therapy*, 38.
8. Rebecca Jorgensen, "Hold Me Tight for Therapists and Their Partners Couples Workshop," *Hold Me Tight Training Manual*, 2014.
9. Ellie Lisitsa, "The Four Horsemen: Criticism, Contempt, Defensiveness, and Stonewalling," The Gottman Institute, April 23, 2013, https://tinyurl.com/jfnk7xf.
10. Johnson, *Emotionally Focused Couple Therapy*, 39.
11. John Bowlby, *Attachment and Loss*, vol. 2, *Separation* (New York: Basic Books, 1973), 406.
12. Johnson, *Emotionally Focused Couple Therapy*, 37.

13. Stan Tatkin, *Wired for Love: How Understanding Your Partner's Brain and Attachment Style Can Help You Defuse Conflict and Build a Secure Relationship* (Oakland, CA: New Harbinger, 2011).
14. You can find the questionnaire at: www.acestudy.org/the-ace-score.html.
15. Laura Starechescki, "Can Family Secrets Make You Sick?," *All Things Considered*, NPR, March 2, 2015, https://tinyurl.com/ycqgrqdr.
16. Starechescki, "Can Family Secrets Make You Sick?," https://tinyurl.com/ycqgrqdr.

Chapter 5: When Trust Is Betrayed: Child Sexual Abuse Trauma

1. "National Statistics on Child Abuse," National Children's Alliance, https://tinyurl.com/y7n8optv.
2. Darkness to Light is a nonprofit committed to empowering adults to prevent child sexual abuse. The organization is guided by its vision to create a safer world for kids. See "Child Sexual Abuse Statistics," Darkness to Light, https://tinyurl.com/y9rwrbbu.
3. Bessel van der Kolk, *The Body Keeps the Score: Brain, Mind, and Body in the Healing of Trauma* (New York: Penguin Books, 2014), 55.
4. Van der Kolk, *The Body Keeps the Score*, 59.
5. Ellen Bass and Laura Davis, *The Courage to Heal: A Guide for Women Survivors of Child Sexual Abuse*, 4th ed. (New York: HarperCollins, 2008), 25.
6. Adapted from "The Red Flags of Grooming Behavior," Darkness to Light, May 8, 2014, https://tinyurl.com/y8pywckh.
7. In October 2017, the Me Too movement (using the tag #MeToo and other tags) was started by victim/survivors of sexual harassment and assault following public reports of sexual misconduct by several prominent public figures.
8. Laura Davis, *Allies in Healing: When a Person You Love Was Sexually Abused* (New York: HarperCollins, 1991).
9. An excellent book on learning masturbation is *Sex for One: The Joy of Selfloving* by Betty Dodson, PhD, originally published in 1974, re-released with pictures and expanded content in 1996 (New York: Three Rivers Press).

10. Rita Nakashima Brock and Rebecca Ann Parker, *Proverbs of Ashes: Violence, Redemptive Suffering, and the Search for What Saves Us* (Boston: Beacon, 2001), 146.

Chapter 6: When Uprooted: Immigration Heartbreak

1. S. Lee and J. Chang, "Mental health status of the Hmong Americans in 2011: Three decades revisited," *Journal of Social Work in Disability and Rehabilitation* 11, no. 1 (2012): 55–70. Lee and Chang studied the mental health status among Hmong refugees in the US and found that one in three fit the criteria for having a trauma-related mental health disorder.
2. Jason Ostrander, Alysse Melville, S. Megan Berthold, "Working with Refugees in the U.S.: Trauma-Informed and Structurally Competent Social Work Approaches," *Advances in Social Work* 18, no. 1 (Spring 2017): 66. The CARA Family Detention Pro Bono Project is a partnership of four organizations: Catholic Legal Immigration Network, Inc. (CLINIC), American Immigration Lawyers Association (AILA), Refugee and Immigrant Center for Education and Legal Services (RAICES), and the American Immigration Council (Council). Since April 2015, CARA has provided legal counsel and representation to several thousand immigrants.
3. Ostrander et al., "Working with Refugees," 67.
4. Jamie Ducharme, "'What This Amounts to Is Child Abuse': Psychologists Warn against Separating Kids from Their Parents," *Time*, June 19, 2018, https://tinyurl.com/ydxts9gk.
5. Ron Nixon, "Federal Agencies Lost Track of Nearly 1,500 Migrant Children Placed with Sponsors," *New York Times*, April 26, 2018.
6. Reggie Thompson, "Who's Really Crossing the U.S.-Mexico Border?" *Forbes Magazine Online*, May 2, 2017, https://tinyurl.com/yaqyycyw.
7. Lindsay M. Harris (American Immigration Council), Karen S. Lucas (American Immigration Lawyers Association), Ashley Feasley (Catholic Legal Immigration Network, Inc.), and Amy Fischer (Refugee and Immigrant Legal and Educational Services), Letter to Department of Homeland Security on March 28, 2016, AILA Doc. No. 16032961.

8. Tori Rodriguez, "Descendants of Holocaust Survivors Have Altered Stress Hormones," *Scientific American*, March 1, 2015, https://tinyurl.com/yd2ltl8l.
9. Rodriguez, "Descendants of Holocaust Survivors."
10. Rita Nakashima Brock and Rebecca Ann Parker, *Proverbs of Ashes: Violence, Redemptive Suffering, and the Search for What Saves Us* (Boston: Beacon, 2001), 53.
11. Brock and Parker, *Proverbs of Ashes*, 55.
12. Brock and Parker, *Proverbs of Ashes*, 63.

Chapter 7: When Death Comes Suddenly: Gun Violence

1. Jason Hanna, Madison Park, Emanuella Grinberg, and Steve Almasy, "School Shooter Will Offer to Plead Guilty, Public Defender Says," CNN, February 17, 2018, https://tinyurl.com/y7xewwr3.
2. John Woodrow Cox and Steven Rich, "No, There Haven't Been 18 School Shootings in 2018. That Number Is Flat Wrong," *Washington Post*, February 15, 2018, https://tinyurl.com/ycufwu6m.
3. Alexandra Sifferlin, "Why Teenage Brains Are So Hard to Understand," *Time*, September 8, 2017, https://tinyurl.com/ybmqqeqm.
4. Lamya Khoury, Yilang L. Tang, Bekh Bradley, Joe F. Cubells, and Kerry J. Ressler, "Substance use, childhood traumatic experience, and Posttraumatic Stress Disorder in an urban civilian population." Wiley-Blackwell Open Online Journal: Depression and Anxiety. 2010 Dec. 27 (12), https://tinyurl.com/yc4o2d2q.
5. "Statistics on Youth Gun Violence & Gun Access," in "Statistics: Do Gun Laws Work?," Giffords Law Center to Prevent Gun Violence, https://tinyurl.com/y8mqqqyq.
6. Elisabeth Kübler-Ross, *On Death and Dying* (New York: Simon & Schuster, 1969).
7. Minerva G. Carcaño, "Lenten Meditation on Violence Caused by Firearms," California-Nevada Annual Conference, The United Methodist Church, March 2, 2018, https://tinyurl.com/ybcwhbma.
8. Sue Klebold, *A Mother's Reckoning: Living in the Aftermath of Tragedy* (New York: Crown Books, 2016).

9. Gregory Gibson, "A Message from the Club No One Wants to Join," *New York Times*, February 17, 2018, https://tinyurl.com/yajjjs5f.
10. Molly Pahn, Anita Knopov, and Michael Siegel, "Gun Violence in the US Kills More Black People and Urban Dwellers," The Conversation, November 8, 2017, https://tinyurl.com/y73gd7dc.
11. "Gun Violence by the Numbers," Everytown for Gun Safety, https://tinyurl.com/gmn6apt.
12. To study this more fully, see Kelly Brown Douglas, *Stand Your Ground: Black Bodies and the Justice of God* (Maryknoll, NY: Orbis, 2015).
13. John Richards, "The Theology of Suffering and Reformed African Americans," The Witness, February 19, 2016, https://tinyurl.com/yawqrkvy.
14. Deborah Epstein and Kit Gruelle, "Should an Abused Wife Be Charged in Her Husband's Crime?," *New York Times*, Op-Ed page, March 13, 2018.
15. Rebecca Ann Parker, "Away from the Fire: Rebecca's Story," in Rita Nakashima Brock and Rebecca Ann Parker, *Proverbs of Ashes: Violence, Redemptive Suffering, and the Search for What Saves Us* (Boston: Beacon, 2002), 31.
16. Susan B. Sorenson, "Guns in Intimate Partner Violence: Comparing Incidents by Type of Weapon," *Journal of Women's Health* 26, no. 3 (March 2017): 249–58, https://tinyurl.com/ybd55cy4.
17. Sorenson, "Guns in Intimate Partner Violence," 249.

Chapter 8: Becoming Spiritually Whole Again

1. Robert Grant, *The Way of the Wound: A Spirituality of Trauma and Transformation* (Oakland, CA: Self-published, 1996), 70.
2. Rebecca Ann Parker and Rita Nakashima Brock, *Proverbs of Ashes: Violence, Redemptive Suffering, and the Search for What Saves Us* (Boston: Beacon, 2002), 44–45.

Chapter 9: Next Steps in Healing

1. Barbara Brown Taylor, *Leaving Church: A Memoir of Faith* (San Francisco: HarperCollins, 2006), 149–50.

2. Barbara Markway, "Is your therapist trauma informed and why it matters," *Psychology Today*, December 29, 2015, https://tinyurl.com/y9dnobs7.

Chapter 10: Rediscovering Hope

1. Olga Khazan summarizes studies on exercise and antidepressants in "For Depression: Prescribing Exercise before Medication," *The Atlantic*, March 24, 2014, https://tinyurl.com/y8dcwnxn.
2. Read more about the sleep-disrupting problems of blue light at https://tinyurl.com/yagaq4yc.
3. Rick Hanson, *Hardwiring Happiness: The New Brain Science of Contentment, Calm, and Confidence* (New York: Harmony Books, 2013), xxv.
4. Peter Levine, *Healing Trauma: A Pioneering Program for Restoring the Wisdom of Your Body* (Boulder, CO: Sounds True, 2008), and other books.
5. My favorite site for brief meditations is found at https://www.headspace.com/.
6. Barbara Brown Taylor, *Learning to Walk in the Dark* (New York: HarperOne, 2014), front cover flap.
7. As a resource for a deeper look at traumatic war wounding, here are two books on recovery after moral injury. Rita Nakashima Brock and Gabriella Lettini, *Soul Repair: Recovering from Moral Injury After War* (Boston: Beacon, 2012). And see also David Wood, *What Have We Done: The Moral Injury of Our Longest Wars* (New York: Hachette, 2016).
8. Mary Beth Williams and Soili Poijula, *P.T.S.D. Workbook: Simple, Effective Techniques for Overcoming Traumatic Stress Symptoms* (Oakland, CA: New Harbinger, 2016).